PREHISTORIC ARIZONA

by Ernest E. Snyder

Professor Emeritus
Arizona State University

Golden West Publishers

Cover design by Bruce Robert Fischer/The Art Studio

Photographs by the author, Ernest E. Snyder

Front cover: Montezuma Castle

Inside front cover: Canyon de Chelly

Back cover: Tuzigoot National Monument

Physical hazards may be encountered in visiting areas of Arizona, particularly old mining
localities. Land ownerships and road conditions change over the years. Readers should take
precautions and make local inquiries, as author and publisher cannot accept responsibility
for such matters.

Library of Congress Cataloging-in-Publication Data

Snyder, Ernest E.
    Pre-historic Arizona.

    Bibliography: p.
    Includes index.
    1. Indians of North America--Arizona--Antiquities.
2. Arizona--Antiquities. I. Title.
E78.A7S68 1987   979.1'01   87-25217
ISBN 0-914846-32-9

Printed in the United States of America

Golden West Publishers
4113 North Longview Ave.
Phoenix, AZ 85014, USA

CONTENTS

INTRODUCTION

My initiation into the mysteries and excitement of pre-historic Arizona came about through a fortuitous happening several decades back. My young sons had received small rifles for Christmas and there was nothing to do but get out and do some shooting.

I took them to an area just south of Phoenix where, seemingly, everyone goes to shoot at bottles and cans. This was at the base of South Mountain (indicated on maps as the Salt River Mountains). Here, at the mouth of a small canyon, the boys were able to expend their complete supply of ammunition with more or less abandon. We then walked a short distance up the canyon to a point where we saw, high up on the west wall, the likeness of an antlered deer inscribed in the rock.

To me, it was beautiful and from somewhere within the dim recesses I knew that this was the work of an early resident some six or more centuries ago. We went a bit farther into the canyon and discovered a boulder near the wash with pictures

Antlered deer and bighorn sheep from South Mountain

of several bighorn sheep and more deer marching across the surface. I immediately became an amateur archaeologist. Returning a week or so later to photograph the petroglyphs, I was distressed to see that someone had pocked the rock in and around the deer with rifle shots.

As time went on, I visited South Mountain often and discovered many more prehistoric petroglyphs. My interest in this area eventually led to two grants from Arizona State University to locate, map and photograph all of the South Mountain petroglyphs and other sites throughout the Salt and Gila river basin.

One cannot journey far within this state without encountering evidence of our heritage from prehistoric times. Grand Canyon is an open book whose pages reveal a record (incomplete but comprehensible) of a billion years of the geologic history of the earth. Petrified Forest National Park preserves fossil trees and animal remains that lived here more than 200 million years ago. Dozens of museums and national parks and monuments display artifacts and structures produced by early Americans going back perhaps 25,000 years before the Spanish explorers set foot on what is now Arizona.

Take a stroll in the desert, the mountains, the canyons or high plateau. Sooner or later you should find an arrow point (probably broken), a ring of stones on the ground, an unrecorded masonry ruin, a piece of broken pottery, or a scatter of chips of obsidian, agate or chert where some unknown and long ago artisan fashioned weapons, utensils or tools from the only suitable material then known—stone. Or you might discover a petroglyph of an antlered deer or a bighorn sheep!

There are few other regions of the world so rich in protected and unprotected evidence of bygone centuries. It is always a thrill for me to come upon an unexpected artifact, ruin or significant geologic feature in museum, park or in the field. The particular emotion generated by an exciting discovery is alive in most of us.

In a brief informational volume such as this, it obviously is impossible to deal in depth with every aspect of the subject. I have tried to include the highlights of each prehistoric culture without an excess of detail. For more information about prehistoric Arizona, the reader is referred to the *Suggestions For Further Reading.* Most of these sources can be found in libraries and bookstores.

With regard to places to visit, I have listed only those that can be reached in the family car on surfaced or improved unpaved roads.

Days and times when ruins and museums are open to the public and admission charges are current only as of the publication date of this book.

FOR YOUR INFORMATION

The Archaeological Resources Protection Act of 1979:

Congress enacted this legislation in an effort to further minimize the destruction of archaeological sites by amateur and commercial pot hunters on public and Indian lands.

Briefly, the Act states that no person may excavate, remove, damage, or otherwise alter or deface any archaeological resource located on public or Indian lands unless a permit has been issued by appropriate authority.

Also, no person may sell, purchase, exchange, transport, receive, or offer to sell, purchase, or exchange any archaeological resource if such resource was removed from public or Indian lands.

The law provides for violators to be fined up to $100,000 and/or be imprisoned for up to five years.

Please take heed!

CHAPTER 1

VERY ANCIENT ARIZONA

What is *prehistoric?* The Spanish explorers arrived in Arizona and the Southwest in about 1540. Since they made oral and written reports of their journeys and discoveries, any time before 1540 is considered prehistoric.

The first non-Indians to enter what is now Arizona were the Spanish priest-explorer Fr. Marcos de Niza and an accompanying Black slave named Estevan. This was in 1539. Estevan, who seemingly moved faster than de Niza, was killed by the Indians at Zuni. Upon hearing this, de Niza hastily returned to Mexico. He re-entered Arizona and New Mexico with Coronado in 1540 and this time made it to Zuni.

On a rocky hillside at the east end of South Mountain near Phoenix is an inscription (a petroglyph, actually) possibly

The Marcos de Niza inscription on the east end of South Mountain, Phoenix

placed there by Fr. Marcos de Niza in 1539. There is convincing evidence that the inscription is a fake but not enough to prevent the City of Phoenix from placing a protective steel grating over the inscribed rock. You may visit the site and decide for yourself as to the authenticity. On my last visit there, the 1539 numerals were no longer legible— despite the protective grillwork. Go south on I-10 to the Baseline Road exit. Follow directions on map to the de Niza rock and Hohokam prehistoric petroglyphs.

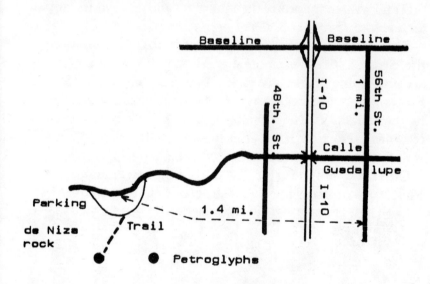

FIGURE 1. Marcos de Niza site map.

Prehistoric, I suppose, could go all the way back to the origin of the earth and the rest of the solar system. For our purposes, however, there is no need to regress quite so far. Some readers may wish to know how the state got this way it is and has been for the past 20,000 or so years. Thus, this chapter deals with the processes that produced the present land forms. (An account of present physiographic provinces, biotic communities, geology, vegetation, natural resources, etc., of Arizona are detailed in Snyder, **Arizona Outdoor Guide,** 1985, Golden West Publishers, Phoenix.)

Let us consider the origins of the present physiographic provinces of the state. These and the resultant and related climates and biotic communities strongly influenced the development of the prehistoric Americans who occupied the area for about 25,000 years prior to 1540 AD.

A physiographic province (sometimes called a geologic province or area) is a region of the earth's surface whose

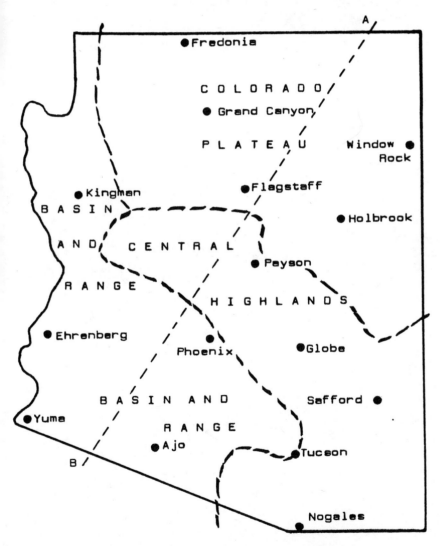

FIGURE 2. Physiographic provinces of Arizona.

landforms are more or less uniform within that region but are different enough from those of adjacent areas to permit casual recognition of the several provinces. Concerned authors have subdivided Arizona into from two to seven provinces. For our purposes here, we shall be satisfied with three: (See Figure 2)

- **COLORADO PLATEAU**
- **CENTRAL HIGHLANDS (or Mountain Province)**
- **BASIN AND RANGE**

During the past six or eight hundred million years, what is now Arizona has spent a considerable amount of time

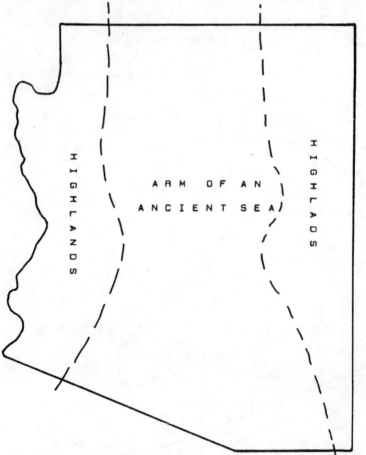

FIGURE 3. Portions of Arizona have been beneath the sea and elevated above sea level numerous times during the past several billion years.

Colorado Plateau rock layers along Oak Creek near Sedona.

beneath an arm of the ocean that extended northward into present-day Canada and Alaska. Land masses existed to the east and west of this relatively narrow body of water. Weathering and erosion from these highlands deposited layers of clay, lime, sand and gravel in the sea and material of this nature is now revealed in the Colorado Plateau. But, now it is solid rock: shale, limestone, sandstone and gravel conglomerates.

At times during these millions of years, the sea disappeared as the area was uplifted by tremendous forces operating beneath and within the underlying crust of the earth. As the water drained away, rain and snow fell, drainage systems were established and erosion removed thousands of feet of the sedimentary rock. During times of subsidence, more material was brought in and younger layers were deposited atop the remains of the older ones.

The Colorado Plateau Province

In the 20th century AD a vertical mile of these rock layers is revealed in Grand Canyon in northern Arizona. But, because of the events just related, the record is incomplete. Even so, a billion years of earth history is represented. Someone has calculated that if the Grand Canyon contained a complete record of those one billion years, it would have to be 180 miles deep! **How would you like to ride a mule down into a canyon that deep!**

Arizona and the entire Colorado Plateau region is undergoing a period of uplift. The area is very slowly but certainly being elevated to ever higher positions above sea level. The Colorado Plateau can be likened to a gigantic stone layer cake making up roughly the northeastern two-fifth of the state and extending far into Utah, Colorado and New Mexico. (See Figure 2.) The "cake" is frosted with deposits of dark volcanic rock over many square miles in the Flagstaff-

Large cinder cone near Show Low.

Williams area and, in the east, in the neighborhood of Show Low and Springerville. These deposits of lava, ashes and other volcanics that have penetrated the plateau sedimentary formations from below, are thousands of feet thick in some places. The volcanic San Francisco Peaks near Flagstaff, for example, reach about 6,000 feet above the sedimentary rocks of the plateau surface. (See Figure 4.)

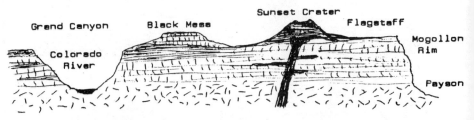

FIGURE 4. Highly-generalized cross-section along line "A-B" in Figure 2 (altered somewhat to include the Grand Canyon). Not to scale; vertical development greatly exaggerated.

San Francisco Peaks near Flagstaff.

This gigantic cake is incised in many places by the drainage systems that have developed during the most recent emergence of the area above the sea. The Colorado River and its tributaries have carved fantastic canyons throughout the region. Geologists think that this development has taken only about 20 million years—a mere blink of the eye as geologic time is reckoned. (By way of contrast, dinosaur remains have recently been discovered in Petrified Forest National Park that are approximately 225 million years old.)

The elevation of the Colorado River in the depths of Grand Canyon is about 2,500 feet above sea level. It is thought that the river has been cutting downward at about the same rate that the plateau region is being elevated. In other words, the river has been at roughly the same elevation since it assumed its present course.

The southern edge of the Colorado Plateau is an escarpment that ranges from a few hundred to several thousand feet in height and extends across the state from near Kingman southeastward into New Mexico. The Rim (or, as it is known in the central part, the Mogollon Rim) exposes the southern edge of the Colorado Plateau and is the boundary between that province and the Central Highlands Province.

Despite what many people think, the Rim is not the result of a gigantic fault—a splitting asunder of the crustal rocks. Rather, it was formed by the headward erosion of the land by streams that are the headwaters of the Salt and Gila river systems of the southern provinces of Arizona. As weathering and erosion removes the softer, less resistant lower layers, the harder rock above breaks away and tumbles down the steep slopes. Fossils found in the lower formations of the rim are about 350 million years old. Compare this with the 225-million-year-old fossils in Petrified Forest National Park. The latter are in much younger rocks located at a higher elevation in our "layer cake."

Canyon de Chelly. One of many canyons cut into the thick layers of rock making up the Colorado Plateau. Note Navajo farmland to right of wash.

The Basin and Range Province

This very distinctive portion of Arizona corresponds to what is referred to as the *Desert* or *Sonoran Desert* region of the state. (See Figure 2). The province constitutes about one-fourth of the area and extends into neighboring Mexico and California.

Typical basin and range ridge and Sonoran desert vegetation east of Gila Bend.

The Basin and Range physiography consists of a series of relatively small mountain ranges that rise abruptly out of the somewhat level basin floor. This floor is largely loose or slightly consolidated gravel, sand, and clay or mixtures of these that have been washed in from nearby highlands to the east and north and from the basin ranges themselves.

In Arizona there are about 40 of these isolated ranges distributed throughout the province. Since they occur somewhat parallel to each other, (and in some cases at right angles to a neighbor), they are believed to be the result of block faulting. Huge portions of the crustal rocks long ago were moved vertically and horizontally and sometimes rotated so that corners and edges of these blocks protruded skyward. Subsequent erosion and deposition produced the ranges and basin floor as we see them today. (see Figure 5)

Mostly unconsolidated material eroded from nearby highlands.

Basin and Range mountains. Corners and edges of blocks.

Largely igneous and metamorphic faulted crustal blocks.

FIGURE 5. Generalized cross-section along line "A-B" in Figure 2 for Basin and Range Province. (Not to scale)

The basin ranges consist of igneous and metamorphic rock usually found in the complex structures underlying the oldest sedimentary formations. Remnants of sedimentary rocks are found at scattered locations in the area. This is an indication that the region at one time probably consisted of great thicknesses of sedimentary rock in the same manner as the Colorado Plateau today, and may have been an extension thereof. These formations subsequently were removed by erosion when broken up by the drastic earth movements that produced the basin ranges. The ranges, of course, were much more resistant to weathering and erosion than were the fractured sedimentary materials.

Province elevations range from about 200 feet above sea level at Yuma to 2000 to above 4000 feet at the summits of the higher mountain ranges. The province is drained by the lower reaches of the Gila, Salt and Santa Cruz rivers, and their tributaries. As we shall see later, these waterways played a vital role in the existence of prehistoric Indians in this harsh desert climate.

The Central Highlands Province

This province lies between the Basin and Range to the south and west and the Colorado Plateau Province to the north and east (see Figure 2). Some physiographers include this area as part of the Basin and Range and in some other cases it is classed as the Mexican Highland Province. For our purposes, however, it is desirable to treat it as a separate entity, since it in no way resembles either the Basin and Range or the Colorado Plateau provinces. It is a distinctive region.

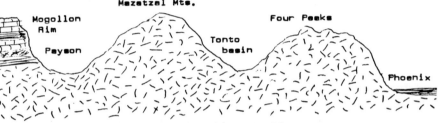

FIGURE 6. Generalized cross-section approximately along line "A-B" in Central Highlands in Figure 2. (Not to scale; vertical development greatly exaggerated.)

Unlike the Basin and Range mountains, those of the Central Highlands are massive developments that are separated from each other only by the canyons and valleys that traverse the area. These mountains were built up primarily through a series of intrusions of granites and basalt into and onto overlying layers of sedimentary rock that may at one time have been a southern extension of the Colorado Plateau.

Elevations vary from 10,000 feet at the summit of Mt. Graham, near Safford, to 2,000 to 3,000 in the lower elevations at the indistinct interface with the Basin and Range province. In the southeastern part of the state, this province overlaps and becomes interspersed with the Basin and Range region. Most of the major Central Highland ranges approach 8000 feet above sea level, whereas basin ranges to not usually exceed 4000 feet.

Some of the larger ranges in this province are: ***Bradshaws, Mazatzals, Sierra Anchas, Pinals, White Mountains, Chiricahuas, Santa Catalinas, Tanque Verdes*** and ***Santa Ritas.*** The area is drained principally by the Salt and Gila river systems and their principal tributaries: Verde, Agua Fria, New, Blue, White, Black, Santa Cruz and San Pedro rivers and Tonto Creek. Some northern portions of the White Mountains are drained by the upper branches of the Little Colorado River.

Because of the wide variation in elevation, climates range from hot desert to alpine cool. Rainfall varies from seven inches per year in the lower elevations to 20 or more inches at the 8,000 to 10,000 foot levels, and temperatures decrease with elevation rise. Consequently, vegetation changes from desert shrub to the Pine-Fir-Spruce-Aspen biotic communities at the upper elevations.

Central Highlands near Apache Lake.

CHAPTER 2

The Earliest Inhabitants

When did the first humans arrive in Arizona? Estimates based on sometimes questionable evidence vary from 10,000 to 25,000 years ago with some rather far-out hypotheses going to 50,000 years BP (Before Present). Substantial evidence from some areas within and not far outside of the state is convincing for the 25,000 years BP arrival time.

Twenty-five thousand years back is the time when the last great Pleistocene (the most recent geologic epoch) ice age started coming to an end. The huge ice sheets that covered large areas of the continents tied up untold millions of tons of the world's water supply. This resulted in a lowering of sea level everywhere several hundred feet. When this happened, the land bridge between Asia and North America at what is now the Bering Strait was broad and dry.

There is little question but that the Mongoloid people from Asia were the forerunners of the Western Hemisphere Indians. Evidence for this lies in the fact that no remains or artifacts of very early man have been discovered in the western world as they have been in Europe, Asia and Africa.

In Arizona there are a dozen or so sites where indications of the earliest emigrants have been discovered. In some cases this evidence is simply a single stone spear point. In others there are crude stone tools, fire pits where food was cooked, and bones of mostly now extinct animals that were hunted by these early people. None of these sites has been developed for public visitation. The main reason for this is that they left no surviving dwelling structures. They probably moved frequently as they followed the game and lived in caves and shelters made of small poles and animal skins. Since they had no beasts of burden, they had to carry everything they owned. Their possessions were simple: weapons, tools and the hides of animals. They did not make pottery and if baskets were used, none has survived.

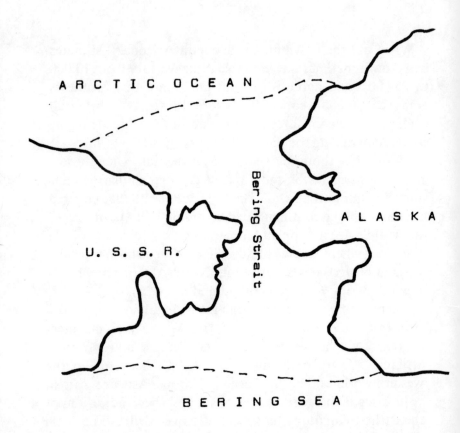

FIGURE 7. *Land bridge at Bering Strait (area between dashed lines) during last Ice Age was about 1,000 miles wide. (Not to scale)*

These first American Indians were basically hunters and existed largely but not entirely on the now extinct animals that inhabited North America at that time. These included prehistoric horses, camels, bison, mastodons, mammoths, ground sloths and tapirs. Because these people occupied most of the continent and were a hunting society, they have been blamed for the extinction of the Pleistocene large animal population. There is, however, no substantial support for this hypothesis.

That they did successfully hunt and consume these animals is without question. Two sites in southern Arizona (and others within and outside of this state) are most convincing. Near Naco, southwest of Bisbee, a kill site was found that contained the bones of a mammoth with eight spear points among them. Apparently the hunters removed the choice cuts of meat but did not bother to recover the weapons points embedded in other parts of the animal. It is believed that this activity took place no less than 10,000 years BP.

The Lehner site is a few miles west and north of Naco and was more than just a kill site. Bones of mammoths, bison and horses with about a dozen associated spear points were found. Two firepits and a number of scrapers, choppers and other stone tools indicate that the camp was occupied for some time. This site also was determined to be more than 10,000 years old.*

It is probable that the Pleistocene hunting culture was spread pretty much over all of North America. Following the last ice age and until about 8000 BP, the climate was quite

*Archaeologists have several methods for determining the ages of artifacts. One used in dating organic remains such as bone and firepit charcoal is called radioactive carbon dating. A definite small percentage of atmospheric carbon in carbon dioxide is radioactive carbon 14. (The stable form is carbon 12). Plants and animals (including you and me) build this radioactive carbon into their structures while living. The isotope changes into a stable element at a precise and unalterable rate (its half-life). By determining the ratio between C12 and C14 in organic remains, scientists can obtain a reasonably good indication of when the plant or animal lived.

humid over the western part of the continent. What are now desert valleys and basins in Arizona had permanent streams and hardwood forests of oak and hickory. As the climate became drier and the Pleistocene game scarcer, the so-called Desert Culture evolved or arrived. Evidence of this development is found throughout the Southwest and into Oregon.

The desert culture was characterized by hunting and gathering. There was probably less reliance on hunting than gathering food from the native plants. Animals that were hunted were deer, antelope, mountain sheep, birds, insects and a multitude of small animals that we would not normally put in the cooking pot. Note the absence of the earlier animals preyed upon by the hunters. It must be assumed that by now these were all extinct—from whatever cause or causes. Plant products included nuts, acorns, berries, roots, bulbs, seeds, cacti, etc. There is no indication of pottery making or of agriculture in this culture.

The Desert Culture in Arizona and western New Mexico is called Cochise and, although there are a number of important sites in southern Arizona, none has been developed for public visitation. The Cochise Culture lasted until around 500 BC.

Mammoth bones with associated weapons points found at the Naco Site. (Photo by Helga Teiwes, courtesy of Arizona State Museum, the University of Arizona)

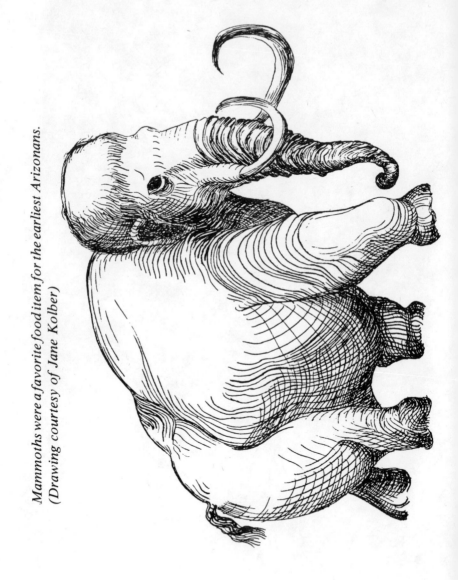

Mammoths were a favorite food item for the earliest Arizonans. (Drawing courtesy of Jane Kolber)

The Lehner site with Mr. Edward F. Lehner, owner, discoverer, and amiable and knowledgeable conservator since 1955.

View of the Rim where Highway Arizona 89 ascends north of Sedona, locally known as "the switchbacks."

CHAPTER 3

Mogollon
(Mountain People)

The Mogollon Culture evolved in the mountainous areas of eastern Arizona and western New Mexico. The name (pronounced "Muggyown") comes from a 16th century Spanish governor of New Mexico. It is believed that the Mogollon originated from the Cochise Culture which formerly occupied the lower elevations of southeastern Arizona, southwestern New Mexico, and northeastern Mexico. These people simply may have moved northward and southward and developed a somewhat different lifestyle.

The major improvement was that the Mogollon developed or adopted agriculture which diminished dependence upon hunting and gathering. This rather radical change may have been stimulated by the fact that the climate in the Southwest was gradually becoming more arid. Streams, lakes and beaver ponds that once supplied an abundance of water were becoming intermittent or were disappearing altogether. Substantial permanent water supplies were to be found at higher elevations where there was greater annual precipitation.

Knowledge of agricultural methods could have come from South or Central America along with seeds of corn, beans and squash. These people did not practice irrigation as did the Hohokam (Chapter 5). They relied upon planting seeds in the flood plains of streams and rivers following periods of high water in the spring or upon summer rains in other areas. (Modern Hopis and Navajos raise crops without irrigation by planting the seed very deep and spacing the hills widely to utilize the sub-surface moisture to greatest advantage.) The Mogollon also built terraces on hillsides to collect and conserve water and soil, and diversion ditches to direct water onto arable areas.

With the advent of agriculture, leisure time became a reality. It was now possible to obtain relatively large amounts of vegetable food easily and to store it for later use. It was no longer necessary to spend virtually all of their time seeking and gathering wild food and hunting animals—although these activities continued on a reduced scale.

The people were able to live year around near their fields. Many advances were made in tool and implement making and dwelling construction. Pottery and basket making began and evolved eventually to a high degree. From shelters in caves and animal skin tents, the Mogollon began living in pit houses—a type of shelter widely used by the southwestern cultures beginning a few centuries BC.

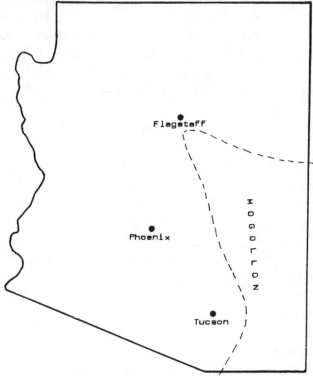

FIGURE 8. The approximate area occupied by the Mogollon Culture in Arizona.

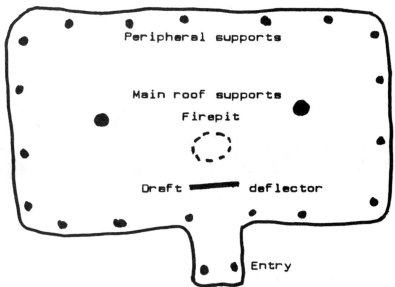

FIGURE 9. Pit house "floor plan" with spots representing holes
where supporting poles were set. Draft deflector was one
or more flat rocks set on edge. The enclosing line is
periphery of excavation.

A pit house was constructed by first excavating the ground
to a depth of from one to several feet. Poles were then erected
to form a framework and branches of trees, brush or reeds
were used to cover the frame. Dirt or mud was used to cover
and thus weatherize the structure. Entry was through the side
in most cases but sometimes through the smoke hole in the
roof. Pit houses ranged in size from eight or ten feet in
diameter to large structures 20 or more feet across—
depending upon the culture and phase. Shapes varied widely:
circular, oval, rectangular, square and irregular. A firepit or
hearth frequently was located near the center of the floor with
a smoke hole above in the roof and a stone slab draft deflector
between the pit and the entry.

During the later stages of the Mogollon Culture (900-
1050), surface structures of stone masonry were built. These
closely resembled the pueblo developments of the Anasazi to
the north. It is highly likely that the Mogollon borrowed these

A reconstructed base frame for a pit house. These heavy posts were set in holes in the floor of the excavation. (See Chapter 5 for photograph of the finished product.)

construction designs and methods from their neighbors. In some cases the Mogollon built cliff dwellings. The most notable of these is at Gila Cliff Dwellings National Monument about 50 miles north of Silver City, New Mexico.

The Mimbres branch of the Mogollon culture deserves special mention because of their beautiful black on white pottery. Fine lines and perfect geometric designs incorporating animals and people make this pottery recognizable in whatever museum you may find it.

As was the case with all of the other prehistoric cultures in the Southwest, the Mogollon people disappeared from their homelands by about 1400 AD. It is possible that the present Zuni Indians of New Mexico are their descendants. The abandonment of their prehistoric homes is discussed in Chapter 9.

There are no developed predominately Mogollon sites in Arizona that are open to the public.

CHAPTER 4

ANASAZI
(Plateau People)

These people occupied the greater part of the Colorado Plateau for a period of about 1600 years (200 BC until about 1400 AD). The word is from Navajo and means, approximately, "The Ancient Ones." Their territory included what is now northeastern Arizona, northwestern New Mexico, southwestern Colorado and southeastern Utah.

The Anasazi evolved through a series of seven cultural steps recognized by most archaeologists. The first three of

Pueblo petroglyphs. People who study prehistoric rock art have had very little success in interpreting these messages on stone.

these are called Basketmaker because of the many baskets discovered in their ruins and burials. There is no convincing evidence that indicates the origins of these people. They may have come from the western Desert Culture for the same reasons that some of the Cochise people moved to higher elevations. Or they could have migrated from the north or east.

In any event, the earliest Basketmakers (who occupied the canyon country after about 200 BC) were hunters and gatherers evolving into agriculturists. Their artifacts and burial remains have been found in caves and rock shelters.* As agriculture became more important, and hunting and gathering were not a daily requirement, time was available for other activities. One of these was the construction of housing closer to the cultivated areas and the gradual elimination of dependence upon natural shelter. Pit houses were the order of the day and these structures became the basic home of the Basketmakers for the next 300 years.

Basketry reached a high degree of excellence and baskets were used as backpacks, storage vessels, water containers (by coating the surfaces with pitch from conifer trees), and cooking vessels. This last was achieved by very close weaving and coatings that would hold water. Food and water were placed in the basket and hot stones were dropped in to

---

*There is a somewhat vague archaeological distinction between cave and rock shelter. Shelters are shallow overhangs mostly in canyons. They were formed when the stream or river was at a higher level and the swirling water with its load of sand and gravel carved recesses in the steep rock banks. Shelters also were formed when quieter weathering and removal of softer lower levels left more resistant layers protruding above. Caves usually are much deeper and were formed as ground water or underground streams dissolved and/or eroded material to create an underground cavity. The uncertainty of definitions arises when trying to decide if a shallow cave is a shelter or if a deep shelter is a cave! And, rarely, caves were formed in volcanic areas when molten lava drained from beneath solidified lava or gases formed and expanded within liquid lava as it cooled.

provide heat for the cooking. Toward the end of the Basketmaker era, pottery was developed or adopted and hot rock cookery faded.

By this time the Basketmaker Anasazi were using the bow and arrow with which to hunt the larger game animals and this, too, made life easier. Leisure time led to improvements in weaving, personal adornment and artistic endeavors such as chipping or painting designs on large rocks or cliffs.

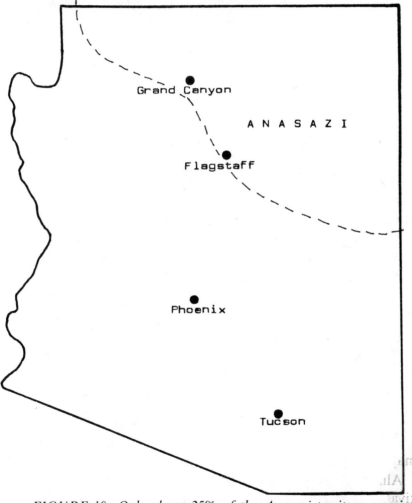

FIGURE 10. Only about 25% of the Anasazi territory was in Arizona. Roughly equal territory was in Utah, Colorado and New Mexico.

There are no Basketmaker sites in Arizona open to the public. The main reason for this is that pit houses do not endure and most people do not enjoy looking at a bunch of holes in the ground.

During the 8th century AD, the Basketmaker Anasazi became the Pueblo Anasazi by the simple process of building their homes and villages of stone rather than sticks and mud. How or where these people learned to construct buildings of stone masonry with log and pole roofs is not known. The only precedent for this sort of thing was to be found in Central and South America.

Since the Basketmaker Anasazi had been trading with other cultures for many years (Abalone shells from the Pacific; parrots and copper bells from Mexico; etc.), it is conceivable that they may have learned of masonry construction of above ground homes from traders; theirs or others. However it came about, pit houses were replaced by pueblo structures after about 700 AD.

At this point it may be desirable to make a distinction between pueblos and cliff dwellings. Pueblo homes and villages were built in the open near streams and rivers and frequently on top of a hill or ridge. Good examples of pueblo construction found in Arizona are at Tuzigoot and Wupatki (Sinagua). Cliff Dwellings were structures built in rock shelters or shallow caves. The overhanging rock formations protected the buildings from the elements. Good examples in Arizona are at Navajo and Canyon de Chelly (Anasazi), Tonto (Salado), and Montezuma Castle (Sinagua). All of these are national monuments and are discussed in detail later.

There must be hundreds of other Anasazi ruins (both pueblo and cliff) in the canyons and mesas of the Colorado Plateau. There is no popular listing or guide to these but some may be located through local inquiry or exploration.

Almost every Anasazi settlement included one or more kivas. These were underground masonry rooms with the roof at or as near as possible to ground level. Most are round or nearly so and were usually entered through an opening in the roof. There was a fire pit with rock slab draft deflectors similar to those found in pit houses. Fresh air entered through a tunnel or a small opening through the wall. Some had built-in seating benches around the periphery and some inside walls were decorated with paintings (murals). Sizes ranged from about 10 to 60 or more feet in diameter.

There can be no question but that kivas were used for religious and/or ceremonial purposes. One indication of this was the sipapu, a small hole in the floor that represented the gateway to the underground origin of the Anasazi ancestors.

A large undeveloped cliff dwelling near Sedona.

One of many pueblo-type ruins in Wupatki National Monument.

Even today the pueblo Indians of Arizona and New Mexico use kivas for social and ceremonial purposes. Presently (as also might have been true in the past) women are pretty much excluded from the kivas. In some Anasazi villages where there were relatively large numbers of kivas for the population, they may have served different clans or families rather than the entire community at once.

If you have witnessed a Hopi Kachina dance, you may have been seeing a descendant of an Anasazi ceremonial. As you watch the male dancers in their colorful masks and costumes emerge from the kiva and march to the plaza, it is easy to imagine that you are at Canyon de Chelly or Betatakin rather than on one of the Hopi mesas. The hours long dance with drums and chanting reinforces the notion that you are viewing something that has its roots in the canyon country a thousand years in the past.

Life was never easy for the Anasazi. Raising corn, beans and squash (pumpkin) on the limited arable land with only hand hoes (flat stones) and digging sticks was nothing less than hard labor. Boulders and smaller rocks had to be moved to clear the ground and build terrace dams. The Indians had no wheelbarrows or carts so all transport of soil and rock had to be in baskets carried by hand from here to there. There were no beasts of burden; the American horse was extinct and European horses and oxen arrived only with the Spanish conquistadors.

The Anasazi did domesticate dogs and turkeys. Dog hair, turkey feathers and rabbit fur were used for weaving (with the help of cotton and other plant fibers) blankets and clothing. There is little or no evidence that dogs and turkeys were used for food. In the later Pueblo stages, loom weaving became quite common.

Pottery and basket making reached a high degree of excellence but may never have competed successfully with Mimbres pottery. Tools, utensils and jewelry were of high quality and surely were used in trade with neighboring cultures. The Anasazi were unsurpassed in their skill at masonry construction as a visit to any of their ruin sites will quickly demonstrate.

Anasazi Ruins and Museums

Petrified Forest National Park, Arizona
    ADDRESS: Petrified Forest National Park, Arizona 86028
    TELEPHONE: (602) 524-6228
    OPEN: Daily 8:00-5:00
    ADMISSION: $5 per car. $2 per bus passenger

Petrified Forest National Park is administered by the National Park Service, U.S. Department of the Interior.

The major attraction at this park is, of course, the amazing accumulation of beautiful petrified logs. There also are some significant prehistoric Indian remains that are of interest.

Petrified Forest N.P. can be reached from I-40 east of Holbrook or from US 180 between Holbrook and St. Johns. The installation is strung out for 27 miles between the two entrances.

If you enter from I-40 (the north entrance) you may wish to visit the Painted Desert Visitor Center to enjoy the 17 minute

A portion of the Rio Puerco ruin in Petrified Forest National Park.

film (shown every 30 minutes) that tells you everything you ever wanted to know about how petrified wood got that way. About the only other thing of interest is the 225 million-year-old skeleton of a Phytosaur—an ancestor of the better known dinosaurs.

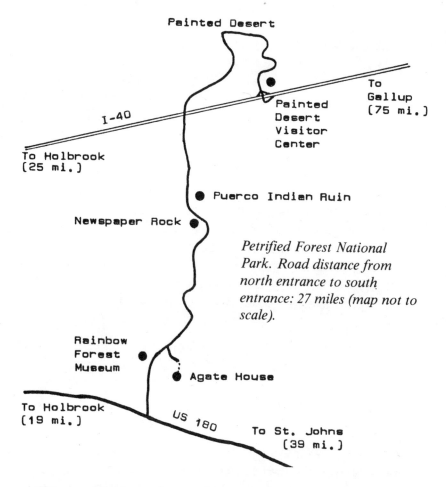

Petrified Forest National Park. Road distance from north entrance to south entrance: 27 miles (map not to scale).

Eleven miles from the north entrance (after an extensive tour of Painted Desert overlooks north of I-40), you arrive at the Rio Puerco Indian Ruin on the east side of the road. Since this northern Arizona region is the fuzzy boundary between the Anasazi and Mogollon cultures, the Park archaeologists refer to the ruins builders only as "Pueblo people."

These ruins have been partially excavated and stabilized. This means that the Park Service did some reconstruction and used concrete instead of adobe on at least the top course of stones. A small squarish sunken room is believed to be a kiva. People are allowed to climb or walk down among the rocks on the south and east sides to see some rather surprising petroglyphs.

About one mile further south is Newspaper Rock (on the west). Instead of walking down steps to get a close look at this concentration of petroglyphs, as could be done before, the Park Service has built a large platform with railing from which we view the rock art almost directly below. If you choose, you can drop quarters in mechanical telescopes for a better look—or save money by bringing your own binoculars.

About 15 miles further along (on the left), you can drive to the trail heads for the Long Logs and Agate House. The latter is a partially reconstructed (restored) pueblo ruin.

Finally, in the same neighborhood, Rainbow Forest Museum has a small display about the Prehistoric Indians. Here we learn that there are about 300 separate ruins in the Park. Do not miss the famous mountain lion (cougar) petroglyph near the other display—impressive.

Canyon de Chelly National Monument, Chinle
ADDRESS: P.O. Box 588, Chinle, AZ 86503
TELEPHONE: (602) 674-5436
OPEN: Daily 8:00-5:00
ADMISSION: No fee area. Free campground.

Canyon de Chelly (pronounced "Shay") National Monument is administered by the National Park Service, U.S. Department of the Interior. This is a unique situation because title to the 130 square miles within the Park remains with the Navajo Nation. Only the maintenance, administration and programming are Park domains. This is why you will find Navajo Indians living and farming all over the place and the Park Service places great emphasis upon respecting the rights and privileges of the property owners. With the exception of the White House Ruin trail, any travel by any means down in the canyon must be with Indian guides. Without doubt, the best way to "explore" the canyon is by large four- and six-wheel drive vehicles with Indian guides. All-day and one-half-day tours leave Thunderbird Lodge at 9:00 and 2:00 daily. Fees are reasonable.

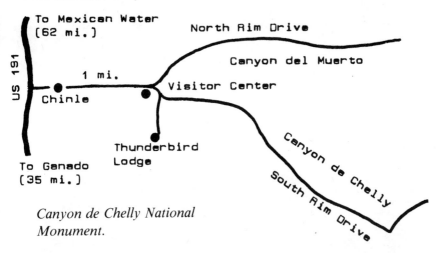

Canyon de Chelly National Monument.

The next best way is to take your car over the south and/or north Rim Drives where numerous overlooks afford good views of the canyon and the Anasazi cliff dwelling ruins near the canyon floor. The North Rim Drive actually is Indian Route 64 that leads to Tsaile and Window Rock, and parallels the northern branch of Canyon de Chelly—Canyon del Muerto (Canyon of the Dead).

The only unguided hike you can take into the canyon is to White House Ruin. The trail head is from White House overlook on the South Rim Drive. Expect a fairly strenuous hike: distance round trip is 2.5 miles and the elevation change is 600 feet. Depending upon the time of year, it may be necessary to wade Chinle Wash to reach the ruin. This is a well preserved Anasazi dwelling site and is worth the hike. **Carry drinking water.** A trail guide is available at the Visitor Center.

White House Ruin in Canyon de Chelly.

The Visitor Center has displays of Basketmaker and Pueblo Anasazi artifacts. Several good reproductions of pictographs and petroglyphs. Accommodations are available at Canyon de Chelly Motel in Chinle (Chin-lee) and Thunderbird Lodge south of the Visitor Center. There is a cafeteria at the lodge.

Navajo National Monument, Tonalea
ADDRESS: HC63, Box 3, Tonalea, AZ 86044-9704
TELEPHONE: (602) 672-2366
OPEN: Daily 8:00-9:00
ADMISSION: No fee area. Free campground.

Navajo National Monument is administered by the National Park Service, U.S. Department of the Interior. This is another installation on Navajo land (see Canyon de Chelly, NM).

This monument protects two major Anasazi cliff dwellings in the Tsegi Canyon area. Betatakin is located in a large alcove or rock shelter and can be viewed by walking about one-half mile on Sandal Trail to an overlook. There is a telescope (no quarters required) so that you can see details of the ruin. Binoculars recommended. This is an easy walk since the trail is paved, washes are bridged and the change in elevation is insignificant. Summer ranger conducted hikes are made into this ruin. Two miles round trip and the elevation change is about 700 feet. Keep in mind that the elevation here is about 7300 feet above sea level.

Keet Seel, one of the larger and best preserved ruins in the Southwest, can be reached only by an eight-mile (one-way) hike or horseback trip during the summer months only. Reservations for these trips must be made several months in advance at the address or telephone number listed above.

The Visitor Center offers a fine five-minute slide show. An unusual collection of pottery is on display courtesy of the Museum of Northern Arizona. A two room Anasazi family

Betatakin Ruin in Navajo National Monument. The ruin is under the rock shelter, but is difficult to distinguish in the photograph because of the distance involved.

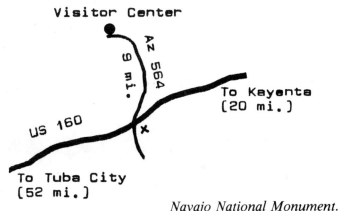

Navajo National Monument.

dwelling has been constructed inside the center and is complete with a small courtyard in which are located three metates in mealing bins—a social "grinding center."

Tusayan Ruins and Museum, Grand Canyon
ADDRESS: Grand Canyon National Park,
           Grand Canyon, AZ 86023
TELEPHONE: (602) 638-7888
OPEN: 7:30-5:00 Summer. 9:00-4:30 Winter.
ADMISSION: Admission fee to Park. Museum no fee.

Tusayan Ruin and Museum are part of Grand Canyon National Park administered by the National Park Service, U.S. Department of the Interior. The ruins and museum are located about 20 miles east of the South Rim Visitor Center and four miles west of Desert View. The entry drive is well signed and is on the north side of the East Rim Drive.

This is an Anasazi pueblo that is among the almost 2000 ruins found on the canyon rims and below in the depths of the gorge. Tusayan appears to have been little disturbed by excavation, rebuilding or stabilization and is pretty much the way it was found many years ago. There are numerous dwelling units and a large kiva.

The small museum displays Cohonina and Anasazi artifacts found in this general area. There are several Paleo

A portion of Tusayan ruin in Grand Canyon National Park. All of the stones visible here were used in the construction.

Indian figurines made of twigs that have been discovered in caves in the canyon. Ranger guided tours of the ruins are conducted frequently. Additional displays may be seen at the South Rim Visitor Center.

CHAPTER 5

HOHOKAM
(Desert Dwellers)

The Phoenix metropolitan area has spread over the remains of an ancient culture that came into being some 2000 years ahead of Phoenix and expired 500 years before the first Anglo settler camped on the banks of the Salt River. Phoenix was named for the beautiful but mythical Phoenix bird that lived for many years, then burned and arose anew from its own ashes.

Phoenix, of course, did not arise from its own ashes but from those of the Hohokam—literally, because the Hohokam almost always cremated their dead. These people possibly entered the Salt and Gila river basins from northern Mexico and developed a fantastic irrigation and agricultural economy by using water from the Gila River and its tributaries (Salt, Agua Fria, Verde, Santa Cruz, San Pedro and Tonto Creek—See Figure 11).

Looking east along one of the original Hohokam canals near Pueblo Grande. This one is exceptionally large—70 feet wide from bank to bank and probably 15 feet deep.

In addition to the riverine people, there was a desert group that occupied the area mostly south and west of the Gila River. These Hohokam subsisted mostly by hunting and gathering, and practicing some primitive dry land agriculture with minimal water utilization. In some cases they constructed homes and villages using the mostly volcanic rock from the Basin and Range mountains. However, their achievements in arts and crafts and as a highly organized society in no way approached that of their relatives to the north and east.

Hohokam (each syllable is equally emphasized) is a Pima word meaning "those who have gone" or "all used up." There is considerable doubt about when these people first arrived in south central Arizona. Some archaelogists say 300 BC while others vote for a time several centuries later. In any event, they soon began irrigating the desert and raising bountiful (for those times) crops in the rich soil. Corn (maize), squash,

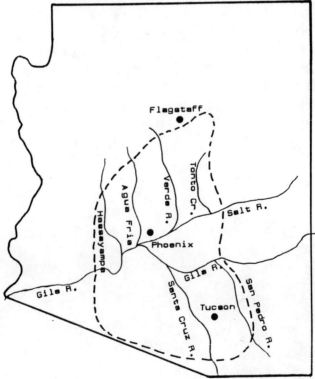

FIGURE 11. Hohokam area within dashed lines includes both desert and riverine cultures.

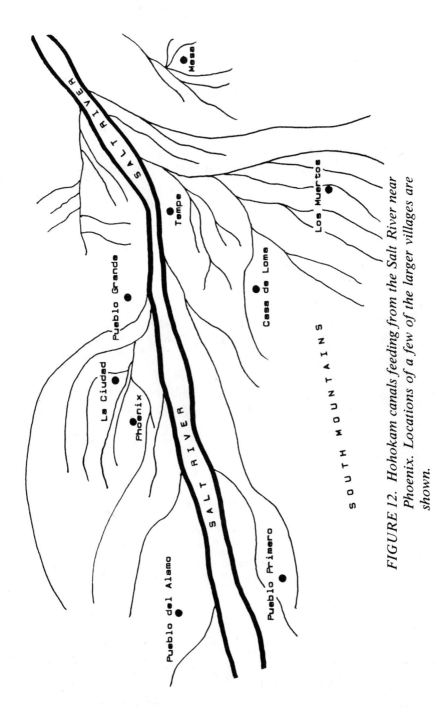

FIGURE 12. *Hohokam canals feeding from the Salt River near Phoenix. Locations of a few of the larger villages are shown.*

beans and cotton were the principal products. Since they could grow several crops per year during the long growing season, they probably did not lack for food. They also hunted animals and collected food from the abundant plant life in the area.

During the 1400 or so years that they occupied the Gila-Salt river system, the Hohokam developed an irrigation system that surely surpassed anything of this nature in the world at that time. In the central Salt River area alone, they constructed more than 300 miles of major canals. This does not include the smaller canals that led into the villages and cultivated fields. (See Figure 12) Main canals began at the river where rock and brush diversion dams sent the water into the canals. Some of these channels were quite large: 40 to 50 feet wide and 10 or more feet deep.

The sheer mass of material that had to be moved is boggling. Especially when we take into account that all of this was accomplished using digging sticks and stone hoes (without handles) and baskets for carrying the soil, gravel, sand and rocks up out of the excavation. Not only was the initial construction approaching the incredible but the canal system had to be maintained—including periodic cleaning and re-excavation.

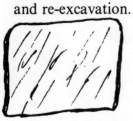  

FIGURE 13. Stone hoes come in many shapes and sizes. They probably were never attached to handles.

The organization and coordination necessary for the planning, construction, maintenance and operation of the system must have required social and civic efforts far beyond what might be expected of a primitive people one step removed from a hunting and gathering existence. One wonders what sort of government these people had. Priestly (shaman) rulers? Chieftains? Kings? Regional councils? Was there a mayor? How about a city manager or public works director? There are no clues.

The Hohokam also irrigated and farmed the Gila River basin centered about the Casa Grande ruin-Coolidge-Florence region. They also advanced far up the tributary rivers and streams both north and south of the core area. Evidence of Hohokam dwellings and settlements are found south of Tucson and in the neighborhood of present-day Flagstaff, also westward to the Hassayampa River and eastward to the Mogollon Rim and Tonto Creek Basin.

For the first 1000 years of their occupation, the Hohokam lived in pit houses (See Chapter 3) which were frequently clustered into loose settlements called rancherias. In some cases the settlements developed into relatively compact towns such as that at Snaketown on the Gila River about 25 miles south of downtown Phoenix. Here there obviously was a well developed social and civic organization.

A major canal from the river ran just above the town and several lateral ditches passed through the living space to provide domestic water for the residents when the canal was

Reconstructed Hohokam pit houses at Gila Indian Center, Heritage Park. Houses were used mostly for sleeping and shelter from storms.

running water. Pit houses were not widely spaced and the sanitary conditions must have been rather rudimentary. There was a trash heap outside the doors of the homes onto which all refuse was tossed or deposited. In many cases two or more families shared a common dump.

These trash mounds have proved to be one of the archaeologist's best sources of information. Since the oldest materials are at the bottom and the youngest at the top, there is a continuous record of the occupation. In addition to all forms of garbage—including plant and animal remains— there is broken pottery, tools and implements, not to mention Hohokam cremation burial urns.

It must be noted here that although Snaketown has been excavated and minutely studied twice in past years, it is presently re-covered with the excavated soil and there would be little to see if you were able to find it. (See Suggestions for Further Reading—Haury, 1986) The site lies a mile or two west of Interstate 10 at milepost 171 but is not accessible from I-10. Snaketown has been recommended and approved as a future National Monument and someday no doubt will be excavated for the third time.

One of the most interesting features unearthed at Snaketown were two ball courts. Upwards of 200 of these have been discovered throughout the Hohokam sphere of influence. Ball courts are usually oval or boat shaped excavations from 70 to 320 feet long and from 40 to 125 feet wide. They varied from 5 to 10 or more feet deep and were sometimes open at both ends. The walls were dirt or stone or both depending, probably, upon location. The large court at Snaketown required the removal of an estimated equivalent of some 3000 truck loads of soil!

Since there is some similarity between these and the ball courts in Central America, they are cited as a strong argument for the original migration of the Hohokam from Mexico. There is, however, no evidence at all that the courts

Unexcavated ball court at Casa Grande.

*Reconstructed stone ball court at Wupatki.
Court is about 50 by 100 feet inside. Inner walls are
five to six feet high. Note openings at both ends.*

were used for the type of ball game played in Mesoamerica. In fact, there is no evidence as to what they were used for. They could have served for some type of game, for religious or ceremonial purposes, or as an open air dance hall—or for some purpose that we have not yet imagined. They apparently fell into disuse during the Classic era because few were built after about 1150. None was found at Los Muertos, for example.

At this time, the Hohokam began building homes of wood and adobe and abandoned many of their pit houses. Snaketown was not occupied during the Classic period. (More about this in Chapter 9). This period of time, roughly from 1100-1450, was when the Hohokam probably reached the peak of their population growth. Homes and rancherias were consolidated into large towns such as Casa Grande, Pueblo Grande and Los Muertos. Also at this time there was a movement into most of the Hohokam core territory of Pueblo Indians from the northeast—the Salado (see also Chapter 6).

This "invasion" appears to have been entirely peaceful and the two cultures apparently existed together in harmony, there being no indications to the contrary. The Salado brought their knowledge of masonry construction but because of the lack of good building stone, resorted to building with adobe. But adobe is dried mud and few of their structures have survived even in this place of little rainfall—about seven inches per year average.

Most of the hundreds of homes and towns that were in the Hohokam core area during the Classic period have disintegrated or have been destroyed by agricultural activities or building development. One of the largest of these, Pueblo de los Muertos (City of the Dead) was completely obliterated. It was located about six miles south of downtown Tempe and two miles west of I-10. The town was more than five miles long and up to one mile wide.

Pueblo Grande in Phoenix also covered several square miles but all that is left above ground is the large platform ("mound") structure on east Washington Street. At the height of Hohokam occupation in the core area, it has been estimated that the population was between 40,000 and 60,000 individuals. Estimations of prehistoric populations are very difficult and especially where cremation was practiced. Other than house or room counts, there is not much to go on. No one knows about family size or longevity. Dwelling counts also are questionable due to the early American practice of rebuilding homes frequently and building anew on top of the old.

Some of the hundreds of petroglyphs at Painted Rock State Park.

The Hohokam were master craftsmen and artists. Examples of their pottery, baskets, shell jewelry, stone figurines and other objects, axe heads, arrow points, etc. may be seen in museums and visitor centers in the area (detailed later in this chapter).

Almost anywhere you go in Hohokamland, you will find their rock art. Inscriptions (petroglyphs) carved or pecked into boulders and rock faces are more than numerous. Reference already has been made to the petroglyphs near the de Niza inscription at the east end of South Mountain Park (Chapter 1). There are many other petroglyphs on South Mountain—especially on the north slopes toward the east end but few of them can be reached without a hike. One of the best examples of Hohokam rock art can be seen at Painted Rock State Park about 25 miles northwest of Gila Bend (see map).

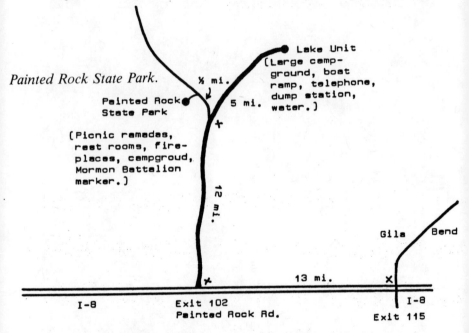

Painted Rock State Park.

Lake Unit
[Large camp-
ground, boat
ramp, telephone,
dump station,
water.]

½ mi.

5 mi.

Painted Rock
State Park

[Picnic ramadas,
rest rooms, fire-
places, campgroud,
Mormon Battalion
marker.]

12 mi.

Gila / Bend

13 mi.

I-8

Exit 102
Painted Rock Rd.

I-8

Exit 115

FIGURE 14. *Painted Rock State Park.*

The name Painted Rock is a misnomer because the figures and designs are not painted on the boulders. In the Southwest, a thin dark coating forms on most exposed rock surfaces. This is called patina or desert varnish. When the material is chipped, pecked, chiseled or scratched away, the lighter colored rock beneath is revealed. The resulting rock art is called a petroglyph. Pictographs are created by applying pigments to the rock surface. Pictographs are quite rare in southern Arizona because they are quickly washed away when exposed to the elements. Pictographs are more common in the northern part of the state where they may be found in caves and rock shelters and are thus protected from the weather.

Let us look at a day in the life of a Hohokam family. Most of these activities would, in a general way, apply to just about any other prehistoric Indian family in Arizona.

Husband

He might spend part of the day farming: planting, weeding, irrigating or harvesting—all by hand or with the inefficient aid of a digging stick or hand held stone hoe.

Hunting: alone or in company with the older son or other men from the village, they might set snares or nets to trap rabbits or other small game. Or go to a nearby mountain range to hunt deer or mountain sheep with spears and throwing sticks (atlatls) or, if after about 700 AD, bow and arrows. If successful, he might trade some meat or hides to the village weapons maker for arrow or spear points to replace those lost or broken.

Building: he could cut saguaro, mesquite or ironwood poles with which to enlarge or rebuild the pit house. The latter two are very hard woods and the labor involved in cutting this stuff with stone axes must have been frustrating, to say the least.

Wife

If the weather is cool, she may clean the ashes from the inside firepit and build a small warming fire. In a shallow pot or on a flat stone, she warms corn cakes baked yesterday along with some leftover wild mutton. This will be the family morning meal. While these are warming, she goes to the nearest village ditch or the river and fills the two water jugs that are kept in the shade cast by the ramada next to the house.

Later she joins several of the neighbor women and they chat while grinding corn and dried mesquite pods. The resulting meal always contains some fine rock dust from the metate and mano that are the grinding implements. This explains why the peoples' molars are ground down as they age.

Before the sun reaches the zenith, she goes along the river and nearby washes gathering willow twigs, yucca stalks and long grass with which to make baskets. Devils claw pods are harder to find but are necessary for the black designs. She teaches some of the older girls in the rancheria to make baskets.

In the afternoon she and the daughter go through the mesquite thickets looking for dead limbs ("squaw wood") to haul home on their burden baskets. Gathering firewood is a daily chore and it seems that they have to go farther from the village every day to find enough for the cooking and warming fires—not to mention the huge amounts of larger pieces needed when there is a death and cremation.

Metates and manos at the Heard Museum, Phoenix. All Arizona cultures used these implements for grinding corn and wild seeds.

Stone tools used by all prehistoric Indians. Upper three are hammer stones used mainly for shaping other stones. Lower right: broken axe probably used as hand held axe or hammer stone. Other two are scrapers or choppers.

They talk of the coming summer when they and the other women and girls go into the desert hills to gather the saguaro cactus fruit. This is a fun time: knocking down the ripe red fruit with long poles made of dead saguaro ribs; bringing loaded baskets of the fruit back to the rancheria to make jelly, syrup and wine is an annual festive time.

Later in the afternoon the wife skins and dresses two rabbits the men have brought in. She saves the skins for future use and throws the entrails on the trash mound. Then she and the girl start a fire to cook the rabbits, some corn cakes and mesquite mush which will be the evening meal with leftovers for the next morning.

Grandmother, who is only about 40 years old, dozes in the afternoon sun during this activity. She has been caring for the baby most of the day and is very tired. Her teeth are bad and

Most household activities took place outside under a sun shelter—a ramada. This one is at the Gila Indian Center, Heritage Park.

arthritis has crippled her until every movement is a major effort.

After dinner the family, excepting grandmother, goes to the plaza to hear the elders of the council report on their recent conference with the other councils up and down the main canal. It will be necessary for all able-bodied people to help with the spring canal cleaning and rebuilding of the diversion dam that had been swept away by the late winter flood.

Soon after the sun has set over the Sierra Estrella, the family moves inside the house and beds down for the night in their cotton and animal skin robes and blankets. The warming coals on the hearth soon are a dim glow and all that can be heard is the occasional howl of a coyote in the distance. Mother remembers just before dozing off that she had planned to spin and maybe weave some cotton today. Oh, well, tomorrow—perhaps.

Hohokam Ruins and Museums

Pueblo Grande, Phoenix

    ADDRESS: 4619 E. Washington Street, Phoenix, AZ 85034

          (See map)

    TELEPHONE: (602) 275-3452

    OPEN: Mon.-Sat. 9:00-4:45. Sun. 1:00-4:45

    CLOSED: Major holidays.

    ADMISSION: Fifty cents over six years of age

Pueblo Grande is administered by the Division of Archaeology of the Parks, Recreation and Library Department of the City of Phoenix.

This installation consists of a Classic period Hohokam platform mound ruin and a museum. Visitors may walk over the ruin on paved walkways. A self-guided trail guide is available and does an excellent job of telling you what you are looking at, on, and around the partially excavated mound. Note (Station 5) the partially excavated and stabilized ball court well to the north. Guided group tours of more than five people can be arranged by calling at least two weeks ahead.

These visitors are walking along the self-guided trail over the mound at the Pueblo Grande platform ruin.

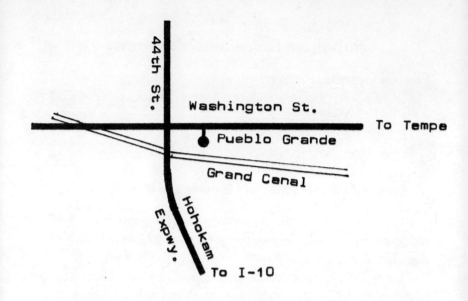

Pueblo Grande.

The museum displays methods of archaeological research as well as excellent arrangements of Hohokam artifacts of all kinds. A reconstruction of a prehistoric adobe structure is on display. A small gift shop is located in the lobby, and offices and laboratories of the Division of Archaeology are located in the museum building.

The Phoenix Chapter of the Arizona Archaeological Society meets here on a regular basis and all interested persons are welcome. Inquire at gift shop for information.

Casa Grande Ruins National Monument, Coolidge
ADDRESS: P.O. Box 518, Coolidge, AZ 85228
      (See map)
TELEPHONE: (602) 723-3172
OPEN: Daily 7:00-6:00
ADMISSION: $3 per car. $1 per bus passenger.

Casa Grande Ruins National Monument is administered by the National Park Service, U.S. Department of the Interior.

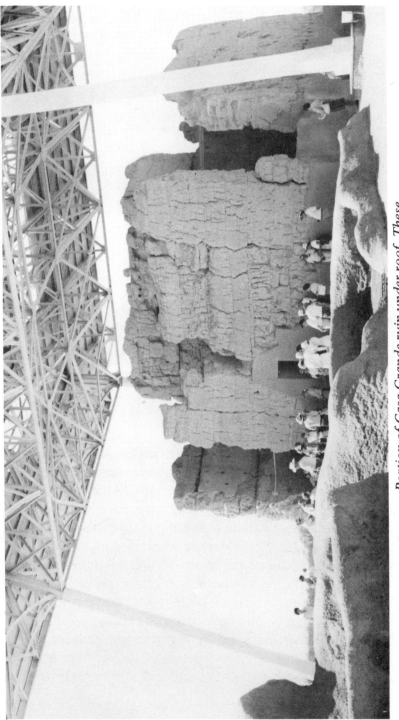

Portion of Casa Grande ruin under roof. These people are enjoying a ranger conducted tour of the installation.

This was a large Hohokam settlement consisting of several compounds, irrigation from the Gila River (85 miles of major canals in the area), numerous unexcavated pit houses, a ball court and a central four-story adobe structure now protected from the rain by a huge steel roof. The adobe construction may have been influenced or engineered by the Salado people who moved into Hohokam territory after 1100 AD (See Chapter 6).

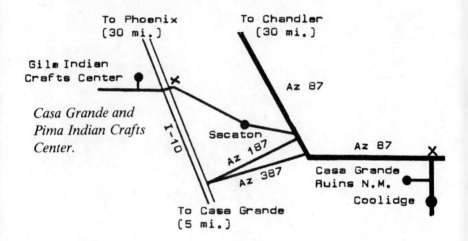

The compounds consisted of numerous adobe rooms apparently used as dwellings and an enclosing adobe wall with only one opening. Archaeologists think that the four-story central sturcture was not used as living quarters but may have served as a ceremonial center and/or as a primitive astronomical observatory. Despite what the early explorers thought, it probably was not used as a defensive bastion.

The visitor museum contains excellent displays of Hohokam artifacts and lifestyle. A low tower just north of the picnic area affords a good view of the ball court.

Guided walking tours led by the resident rangers are conducted at 45 or 60 minute intervals during the winter season.

Gila Indian Crafts Center, Bapchule
  ADDRESS: P.O. Box 457, Sacaton, AZ 85247
        (See Casa Grande map)
  TELEPHONE: (602) 963-3981
  OPEN: Daily 9:00-5:00
  ADMISSION: No charge to museum and crafts center.
        Sometimes charge to Heritage Park.

Owned and operated by the Gila River Indians.

Attractive gift shop offering basically authentic art and crafts from many of the Southwest tribes.

Museum is located in the north end of the gift shop building. Interesting displays of Pima and Hohokam history and culture including a mud and wattle house with ramada (Pima *vato*).

Restaurant has varied menu of Indian, Mexican and Anglo food. Everyone should try Indian fry bread; most people come back for more.

Gila Heritage Park displays replicas of Hohokam pit houses, and Papago and Pima dwellings, among other things. It is well worth the short stroll northwest of the main building.

The Hardy Site, Tucson
ADDRESS: Fort Lowell Park, 2900 N. Craycroft Rd.,
Tucson, AZ
(Mail) Fort Lowell Museum, 949 E. 2nd St.,
Tucson, AZ 85719
TELEPHONE: (602) 885-3832
OPEN: All hours daily
ADMISSION: No charge

The Hardy Site and Ft. Lowell Park are administered by the City of Tucson.

The site itself was a large Hohokam pit house village occupied for some 1000 years. The village covered all of what is now Fort Lowell Park and extended in all directions to cover an area four or five times greater than that of the park. Most of the village is now covered by old Fort Lowell ruins, the Park, and homes and streets that surround the park.

A small portion was excavated by the Arizona State Museum and the outline of one pit house is preserved and a series of 10 explanatory panels were erected at that point. To

The Hardy site in Fort Lowell Park, Tucson.
The posts are in and around the low well that marks
the pit house outline.

reach the display, go to Fort Lowell Park at North Craycroft and Glenn. Drive in the second entrance east of Craycroft on Glenn. Go straight ahead and park in the northeast corner of the tennis courts parking area. You can see the displays across the footbridge and a bit to the left.

A few displays relating to the Hardy site are to be seen in the Fort Lowell Museum located on the west side of the park. This facility is open Wed.-Sat. 10:00-4:00.

Arizona State Museum, University of Arizona, Tucson

ADDRESS: University of Arizona, Tucson, AZ 85721
TELEPHONE: (602) 621-6302
OPEN: Mon.-Sat. 9:00-5:00. Closed some holidays.
    Call for information. Sun. 2:00-5:00.
ADMISSION: No admission charge

The Arizona State Museum is state-owned and administered by the University of Arizona and is located on the campus at the corner of Park and University. Parking is available on the streets and in parking lots west of Park Avenue.

This is one of the finest museums in the region and, although it is in Hohokam territory, it does not deal exclusively with this culture. There is an imaginative display of the archaeology of the cave dwellers, and another concerning the elephant (mammoth) hunters in Arizona.

Toward the rear of the main floor is an exhibit based on a huge cross-section cut from a giant redwood dealing with the method of dating ruins using the growth rings in trees where seasonal variations make the rings prominent enough for study. This science of dendrochronology originated here at the University of Arizona under the aegis of an astronomer, Dr. A. E. Douglass. Tree ring dating, as it is more popularly called, has been an invaluable aid to Southwestern archaeologists.

The mezzanine contains some exhibits of Arizona flora and fauna as well as an extensive collection of Hohokam artifacts. There are also displays emphasizing prehistoric pottery and basketry. There is some emphasis upon the Mogollon on the main floor.

Mesa Southwest Museum, Mesa
ADDRESS: 53 N. Macdonald, Mesa, AZ 85001
TELEPHONE: (602) 834-2230
OPEN: Mon.-Sat. 10:00-5:00. Sun. 1:00-5:00
ADMISSION: $2.50. Ages 5-12 yrs. $1; age under 4 yrs., free
Discounts for students and senior citizens.

Museum is administered by Mesa Parks and Recreation.

A Paleo-Indian exhibit includes mammoth fossils and artifacts from the earliest inhabitants (Chapter 2). In the large prehistoric Indian room are exhibits of: Pottery from 1 AD to present; Salado cliff dwelling home; Real petroglyphs on small boulders; Hohokam pit house; and Hohokam-Salado adobe houses.

This museum has something for everyone. Children especially enjoy the historical geology room including an animated Tricerotops. Emphasis here is on dinosaurs. Outdoor facilities include a pond where children can pan for gold.

The museum is located in downtown Mesa on Macdonald just a block or two north of Main Street.

Arizona State University Anthropology Museum, Tempe
   ADDRESS: Arizona State University, Tempe, AZ 85287
   TELEPHONE: (602) 865-6213
   OPEN: Mon.-Fri. 8:00-5:00. Closed weekends and holidays
   ADMISSION: No charge. Donations welcomed.

This museum is administered by the Department of Anthropology of Arizona State University.

Arizona State University archaeologists excavated about 15 acres of La Ciudad (The City) in central Phoenix ahead of freeway construction. More than 500 acres were not excavated because this part of La Ciudad now lies beneath homes, streets and buildings north and south of the Moreland Corridor (site of a future freeway).

Most of the exhibits deal with artifacts from the dig. The displays are very well done and the viewer obtains a good look at 1000 years of Hohokam life in one of the larger pit house towns in the core area.

If you are not familiar with the ASU campus, you might do well to enter the area from the west and inquire of an officer at the entrance as to where to park and how to find the Anthropology building. The University Art Collection and Museum is in Matthews Hall directly south of the Anthropology building.

Heard Museum, Phoenix
ADDRESS: 22 East Monte Vista Rd., Phoenix, AZ 85004
TELEPHONE: (602) 252-8840
OPEN: Mon.-Sat. 10:00-5:00. Sun. 1:00-5:00.
      Closed major holidays.
GUIDED TOURS: (Sept.-May) Tues. 1:30.
                Sat. 11:00, 1:30, 3:00. Sun. 1:30, 3:30
ADMISSION: $3 adults. $2.50 Sr. Citizens.
              $1 Children and students

This museum is privately endowed and supported by gifts, memberships and admissions.

A boulder at the southeast corner of the building near the entrance to the gift shop and bookstore contains Hohokam petroglyphs. More petroglyphs are on boulders in the Sculpture Court. Numerous metates and manos (milling implements) are in the patio.

This museum has one of the most complete and extensive collections of prehistoric southwestern Indian artifacts in the West. This is equalled only by the fine arts of historic Indians. The hundreds of Kachina dolls from the Barry Goldwater and Fred Harvey collections are on permanent display.

Unexcelled is the *Native Peoples of the Southwest* permanent exhibit. Splendidly displayed, it has an audio-visual orientation area followed by the Hohokam unit *The Desert;* Mogollon, Salado and Sinagua, *The Uplands;* and finally, *The Colorado Plateau.*

Most of the rest of this large museum is devoted to displays of basketry, pottery and contemporary fine arts of many native Americans. Some of these are changed periodically.

Special group tours may be arranged by calling ahead. The Heard is easily found by driving on Central Avenue north of McDowell or south of Thomas. Turn east on Monte Vista. The museum is just a block or two from Central on the north side of the street. There is a parking lot on the east side of the museum. Signs on both sides of Central Avenue indicate where to turn onto Monte Vista.

CHAPTER 6

SALADO
(Salt River People)

No one seems to know exactly where the Salado lived before they moved into some of the upper Salt and Gila river drainage. (Salado is Spanish for salt). It appears likely that they moved down over the Mogollon Rim from the Little

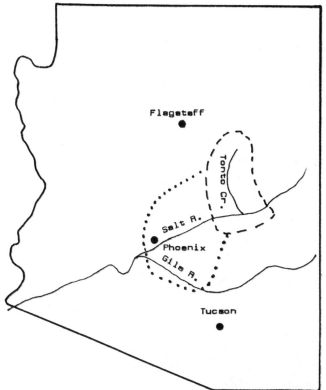

FIGURE 15. Salado country. Dashed line: Tonto Basin and upper Salt River drainage. Dotted line: late expansion into Hohokam core area.

Colorado River area. On the other hand, some have suggested that the Salado people are a melding of Anasazi and Mogollon with some strong Hohokam catalysis.

In any event, they occupied Tonto Basin completely and colonized much of the territory from the lower reaches of the Mogollon Rim to the neighborhood of Globe by 1100 AD. And, as we have seen, they later (1300s) moved into the Hohokam heartland (Figure 15). Actually, a smattering of Hohokam were already in Tonto Basin when the vanguard Salado arrived.

One reason why it has been relatively easy to define the Salado territory is that they produced a distinctive poly-chrome pottery of white, black and red. But they also made undistinguished red ware. Also, unlike the Hohokam who usually cremated the dead, the Salado buried their deceased—frequently under the floors of the living quarters.

Most Salado dwellings were single or several room struc-tures of stone using mud for mortar. They also built large pueblo villages of connected rooms such as the ones at Globe (see descriptions at end of chapter). Most of their homes were close by the land they farmed. The author discovered a small Salado ruin in the Pinal Mountains 25 miles southwest of Globe. The people had made a rock dam (trincheras) that collected water and soil washed down from a small adjacent mountain. This resulted in a "farm" of about one acre of almost level land. The two homes were constructed on a small hill at the edge of the field.

Around 1250 the Salado (or some of them, at least) built homes (cliff dwellings) at considerable distances from their cultivated fields. Many of these have been found in the Mogollon Rim canyons and canyons in the Sierra Ancha Mountains on the east side of Tonto Basin. Just why they made this change is not known for certain. An attractive hypothesis maintains that forerunners of historic warlike Apaches were raiding the Salado farming communities and they were forced to build defensive structures.

Tonto Cliff dwelling ruin near Roosevelt Dam.

It was also about this time that many of these people migrated to the low desert region and took up residence with the riverine Hohokam (See Chapter 5). Tonto National Monument near Roosevelt preserves several of the Salado cliff dwellings (See end of chapter).

Most of the Salado cultural remains near Tonto N. M. are under the waters of the lake behind Roosevelt Dam. The junction of Tonto Creek and the Salt River must have been prime real estate in Salado time. No doubt they learned much from the resident Hohokam about raising several kinds of beans, squash, corn and possibly cotton. The Salt River from that point to where it emerged from the mountains near Mesa, had little to offer in the way of arable land. The route was rocky and precipitous, and has been tamed only in the 20th century by the Salt River Project water storage dams.

Along with all of the other identifiable prehistoric people in Arizona, the Salado abandoned their homes along the upper Salt River and other places and no evidence of their existence elsewhere has been found. The ones that were living among the riverine Hohokam disappeared, apparently, at the same time as the original desert farmers.

Salado Ruins and Museums

Tonto National Monument, Roosevelt
ADDRESS: P.O. Box 707, Roosevelt, AZ 85545
TELEPHONE: (602) 467-2241
OPEN: Daily 8:00-5:00. Trail to lower ruin closed
    at 4:00 for starting up.
ADMISSION: $3 per car. $1 bikers and bus passengers.

Tonto National Monument is administered by the National Park Service, U.S. Department of the Interior. The monument consists of three Salado cliff dwelling type ruins but only the lower ruin is open to casual visitors. The upper ruin (three miles, three-hour hike) must be arranged two days in advance.

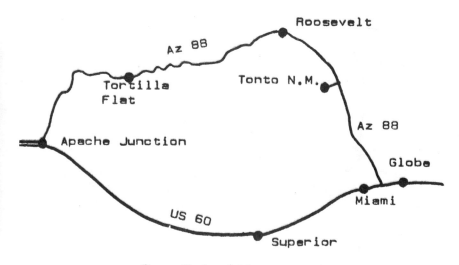

Tonto National Monument.

You have a choice of two routes to this monument. The more scenic and adventuresome way is to take Arizona highway 88 north from Apache Junction (See map). Forty-nine miles of twisting mountain road with steep grades and sharp curves and very few guard rails. Twenty-two miles is unpaved but well graded. To save wear and tear on the car

The Salt River arm of Roosevelt Lake where the Salado farmed and lived. Photo was taken from the trail to Tonto ruin.

brakes and your nervous system, use lowest gear on Fish Creek Hill. Just out of Apache Junction is a highway sign: "No vehicles over 30 feet long." Better believe it.

The other route is longer (about 76 miles) but quite benign. Take U.S. 60 from Apache Junction to the point where AZ 88 intersects between Miami and Globe. Turn north (left) on 88. It is 27 miles to the monument entry road.

The small but well done visitor center tells the story of the Salado and exhibits depict their lifestyle. Numerous artifacts are displayed. Slide show with commentary is worth watching—a good place to sit and rest after your hike to the lower ruins.

Hike up hill to ruin is strenuous but rewarding. Pick up trail guide at desk. Paved trail is about one-half-mile with numerous benches on which to rest. Visitors may enter most of the rooms in the ruin.

Besh-Ba-Gowah Ruins, Globe

ADDRESS: Globe, AZ (No mailing address)
OPEN: 7:00-7:00
ADMISSION: No fee area.

This Salado ruin is owned and administered by the City of Globe. At this writing, the museum building is about 60 percent finished, and reconstruction and stabilization of the ruin is well underway. Much of the work is being done by volunteers from the Arizona Archaeological Society.

Besh-Ba-Gowah (Apache meaning "metal camp") was built beginning soon after 1200 AD and abandoned in about 1400. This large pueblo is unusual in that it was constructed almost entirely of rounded boulders from the nearby streams and washes.

This should be a first-class facility when completed. Even now it is worth the trouble of getting there (See map). At the present time, it shares the grounds of the Globe Community Center which includes game areas and picnic facilities. A pleasant place to stop, look and relax.

Besh-ba-Gowah, a Salado ruin at Globe. Partially restored.

Gila Pueblo, Globe

ADDRESS: Gila Pueblo, Gila Pueblo College, Six Shooter
Canyon Road, Globe, AZ 85501
TELEPHONE: (602) 425-3151
OPEN: Mon.-Fri. 8:00-5:00. Closed major holidays.
ADMISSION: No fee area.

Owned and administered by the Gila Pueblo Community
College, Globe, Arizona.

This ruin is located only about one mile from Besh-Ba-
Gowah and has undergone several radical changes since
1928 when Harold S. Gladwin purchased the site. He hired
Mexican masons to first raze and then rebuild the main
structure. This building with its 57 rooms is now occupied by
the college.

Between 1928 and the present, the ruin has been owned or
administered by Gladwin, the University of Arizona, National
Park Service and Southwestern Monuments Association.

Visitors are welcome at the college. You will be directed to
an inner room where there are several displays of Salado
artifacts. On the southwest side of the building are a dozen or
so excavated and stabilized room walls and some that have
not been excavated.

Gila County Historical Museum, Globe

ADDRESS: 1330 North Broadway,
           P.O. Box 2891, Globe, AZ 85501
TELEPHONE: (602) 425-7385
OPEN: Tue.-Fri. 9:00-4:30. Sat. 10:00-4:00
ADMISSION: No charge.

Mostly historic displays but one room contains some excellent Salado and Apache pottery and basketry. Also an unusual stone hoe and mortar and pestle. These objects were formerly in the lobby of the Dominion Hotel.

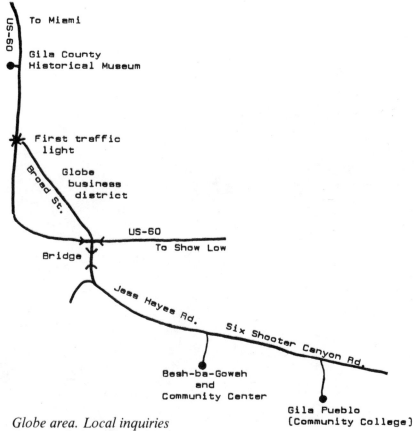

Globe area. Local inquiries may help locate Six-Shooter Canyon Road. (Map not to scale)

Sunset Crater near Flagstaff.

CHAPTER 7

SINAGUA
(Volcano People)

The Sinagua originally lived in the Flagstaff region on the slopes and flats adjacent to the San Francisco Peaks. When the Spanish explorers visited this part of the Southwest, they named these mountains Sierra Sin Agua ("mountains without water") because of the almost total absence of permanent streams or rivers in the immediate area. This condition is due mainly to the fact that the entire region is covered with deposits of very porous lava and volcanic ash. The surface waters sink quickly to the depths. When archaeologists discovered the remains of this culture, they named it Sinagua—"(people) without water."

The layer of volcanic ash deposited over an 800 square-mile expanse when an eruption created Sunset Crater in 1064 has been cited as a boon to prehistoric agriculture there. Precipitation soaked quickly through the ash layer into the soil beneath. Then the ash served as a natural mulch, slowing the evaporation of water and thus made more moisture available to seeds and plants over an extended period. Some archaeologists maintained that this phenomenon was responsible for a brisk movement of neighboring Indians into the area. Others are disputing this hypothesis.

In any event, Anasazi, Mogollon, Cohonina and a few Hohokam did arrive and the Sinagua adopted some of their customs. The most notable thing was that they soon forsook their pit houses in favor of masonry surface structures similar to those of the Anasazi. The almost countless ruins in the Flagstaff area and the Verde Valley attest to this fact. They also adopted the Hohokam ball court of which about a dozen have been located in Sinagua territory. The masonry reconstructed court at Wupatki is a beautiful example.

Population pressures and/or diminishing precipitation may have caused the movement of many of the Sinagua from their volcanic fields to Walnut Canyon and to the Verde River and its tributaries below the Rim during the eleven and twelve hundreds. At Walnut Canyon the people built small dwellings in rock shelters and under ledges in the canyon walls and surface structures a short distance back from the canyon rims.

They cleared and farmed the flat land along the rims and enjoyed the permanent water of the canyon stream. They hunted the game which must have been quite plentiful at the time. Local wild vegetation added to the corn, beans and squash from their gardens. Pinyon nuts, acorns, cactus fruits, pigweed seed, agave stalks, elderberry, currants, yucca fruit and seeds, were some of the vegetable foods gathered.

The lifestyle, ceramics, tools, weapons and utensils were similar to those of cultures already described. It is probable that cotton would not mature here so there must have been a lively trade with the southern Hohokam for this item.

Conditions in the Verde Valley changed over the years for the Sinagua. So many people moved into this area that population pressure alone must have created many problems. In addition to Tuzigoot and Montezuma Castle and Well, there are numerous smaller ruins (both pueblo and cliff) that have been found. The smaller canyons between Oak and Cottonwood creeks contain many cliff dwellings and, as of the present, there are no permanent streams. Several ruins had windows or doors sealed with masonry leaving only a peephole—(or arrow port?). This suggests defensive tactics. Away from the escarpments, pueblo type ruins are found at the very tops of small peaks.

The Sinagua abandoned all of their homes in the early

1400s and have not been detected elsewhere as a definitive culture (See Chapter 9).

Sinagua Ruins and Museums

Wupatki Ruins National Monument, Flagstaff
ADDRESS: HC 33, Box 444A, Flagstaff, AZ 86001
TELEPHONE: (602) 527-7040
OPEN: Daily 8:00-5:00.
Closed Christmas and New Year's Day.
ADMISSION: No fee area.

Wupatki and Sunset Crater are combined for administrative purposes by the National Park Service, U.S. Department of the Interior. The two monuments are connected by a paved loop road that intersects U.S. 89 at two points (See map).

There are more than 1000 Sinagua surface ruins within the monument boundary. Only five are open to the public at this time. The main ruin is an easy walk from the Visitor Center's back door. Note the "amphitheater" and the reconstructed ball court. Do not miss the blow hole near the ball court. This may be the only opening to underground cavities estimated to be seven billion cubic feet. This is equivalent to a building one mile square and 28 stories high! When the outside air is warm (lower pressure), cool air rushes out of the hole. When the outside air is cold or cool (higher pressure) air is forced back into the cavity.

The other four ruins are worthy of attention. None is as large as the main ruin but offer some surprises. Lomaki, for example is not one ruin but three located within shouting distance of each other. All of these ruins are reached by short walks from parking areas.

The Visitor Center has the usual excellent Park Service displays. The ones here naturally concentrate on the Sinagua.

Sinagua pueblo ruin at Wupatki National Monument.

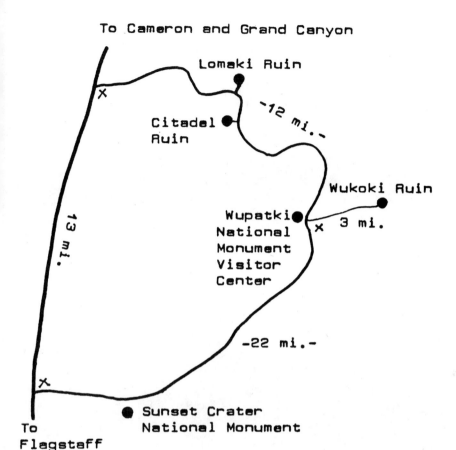

To Cameron and Grand Canyon

Lomaki Ruin

Citadel Ruin

-12 mi.-

Wukoki Ruin

Wupatki National Monument Visitor Center

3 mi.

13 mi.

-22 mi.-

To Flagstaff (12 mi.)

Sunset Crater National Monument

Wupatki and Sunset Crater National Monuments.

Walnut Canyon National Monument, Flagstaff
   ADDRESS: Walnut Canyon Road, Flagstaff, AZ 86004
   TELEPHONE: (602) 526-3367
   OPEN: Daily 8:00-5:00.
       Closed Christmas and New Year's Day.
   ADMISSION: $3 per car. $1 per bus passenger or biker.
   Walnut Canyon National Monument is administered by
the National Park Service, U.S. Department of the Interior. It
is reached from I-40 about four miles from the easternmost
Flagstaff exit. Entry leads three miles to Visitor Center (See
map).

One of the Sinagua ruins on the "island" at Walnut Canyon National Monument.

This group of Sinagua occupied Walnut Canyon for only a few centuries but during this short time they built more than 300 dwellings in the canyon walls. In addition, there are surface ruins on the canyon rim some of which are to be seen just north of the picnic grounds.

Trail guide booklets are available for the hike down to and around the "island" group of cliff dwellings. Heed the warnings about the strenuous climb back up to the Visitor Center. The Center offers good displays of all aspects of the Sinagua culture. A 25 minute video film show is available except during the summer months when the nuseum area is too crowded for good viewing. The Rim Trail is easy walking and informative and affords two splended views of the canyon.

View of Walnut Canyon looking toward the Visitor Center (at upper right). Sinagua Indians built homes under overhanging ledges visible in photo and on the forested top of the canyon rim.

Tuzigoot National Monument, Clarkdale
ADDRESS: P.O. Box 219, Camp Verde, AZ 86322
TELEPHONE: (602) 634-5564
OPEN: Daily 8:00-5:00
ADMISSION: $3 per car. $1 per bus passenger.

Tuzigoot National Monument is administered by the National Park Service, U.S. Department of the Interior. The ruin is in the Cottonwood-Clarkdale-Jerome area and is easily reached from I-17 near Camp Verde (See map).

This is about the largest pueblo type ruin open to the public in Arizona. It was built on the top and slopes of a prominent hill southeast of what is now the town of Clarkdale. Tuzigoot (Apache for "crooked water") Sinagua farmed the land between the hill and the Verde River. The village contained upwards of 100 rooms and was founded, built and abandoned between 1125 and 1400. It was constructed of rounded river rock and unshaped field stones that are subject to quick collapse when protective roofs deteriorate.

The Visitor Center contains interesting exhibits including a large map of Arizona with pottery shards arranged around

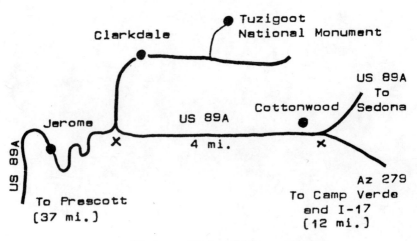

Tuzigoot National Monument.

Tuzigoot National Monument. Sinagua Indians built this large pueblo of river rocks and field stones.

it according to the several prehistoric cultures. It is easy to see how archaeologists are able to identify a ruin site by the broken pottery left behind by the inhabitants. Be certain to see the matched obsidian arrow points and the display about how the Sinagua made beads of stone—some of which are unbelievably tiny.

There is also a reconstructed room in the Visitor Center that houses some of the Sinagua tools, utensils, fabrics and other handicarfts.

Montezuma Castle and Well National Monument, Camp Verde
ADDRESS: P.O. Box 219, Camp Verde, AZ 86322
TELEPHONE: (602) 567-3322
OPEN: Daily 8:00-5:00
ADMISSION: $3 per car. $1 per bus passenger

Although the Castle and the Well are separated by 8.5 highway miles, they are administered as a unit by the National Park Service, U.S. Department of the Interior. There are no facilities at Montezuma Well beyond a small shelter for the ranger on duty. To reach Montezuma Castle, leave I-17 at Exit 289 a few miles north of Camp Verde and follow signs about three miles to the Visitor Center.

This is one of the worst misnomers in the entire Southwest. Montezuma Castle was named by early settlers in the Verde Valley. This ruin is a cliff dwelling, not a castle, and Montezuma was never near the place. But the name persisted and, furthermore, the Well is not a well, it is a spring.

There are many Sinagua cliff dwellings in the Sedona-Verde Valley area but this is one of the largest and best preserved. Visitors are no longer permitted to enter the ruin because of the fragility of the masonry. Suppose that your brick home used mud for mortar and was 700 years old—how well preserved do you think it would be?

Montezuma Castle was built high up in an overhang in the Verde limestone.

The Hohokam came into the Verde Valley around 800 AD and farmed the stream bottom land by using irrigation canals. They lived in pit houses and apparently never bothered with masonry surface structures. Some Sinagua came down from the Colorado Plateau and seemed to live in harmony with the early settlers and adopted their farming methods.

The Visitor Center has a small museum that offers much information about the early Sinagua and Hohokam settlers. These Indians mined salt from an area just southwest of what is now Camp Verde—a valuable trade item. There is an interesting exhibit about poisonous wildlife of southern Arizona.

Take the short walk to view the ruin high up in the cliff. There are explanatory signs and an audio presentation that will enhance your enjoyment.

Montezuma Well

This satellite of the Castle should not be passed up. Turn right at Exit 293 (McGuireville-Lake Montezuma—Rim Rock, etc.) and follow signs about five miles to the Well (See map). About one mile of the road is unpaved but is always in good condition.

This is another Sinagua-Hohokam area and is centered about a sinkhole spring that produces 1.5 million gallons of water each 24 hours. The sinkhole was formed when the roof of a large limestone cavern collapsed untold years ago. The springs are below the present water surface (maximum depth 55 feet) and the water flows out through a cave under the south wall of the "well."

Visitors are free to take the trail down to the bottom and inspect the several masonry dwellings there. Note also the small cliff dwellings near the top of the escarpment on the west side.

The rim trail to the outside outlet near Beaver Creek and the parking lot passes two pueblo ruins. About half-way

Looking west from down by the water, in Montezuma Well. Note cliff dwellings near top of escarpment.

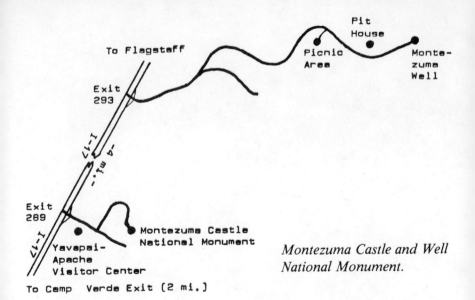

Montezuma Castle and Well National Monument.

between the parking lot and the picnic ground is a large Hohokam pit house floor protected by a modern roof. Parts of the picnic area are irrigated by water from the Well just as the prehistoric Indians watered their corn, squash and bean fields. Do not miss the ancient canal located where the road to the picnic ground comes down the hill. These old canals are lined with calcium carbonate ("lime") because the spring water is loaded with the stuff in solution—so much so, in fact, that no fish can live in the Well.

Museum of Northern Arizona, Flagstaff
ADDRESS: Route 4, Box 720 Flagstaff, AZ 86001
TELEPHONE: (602) 774-5211
OPEN: Daily 9:00-5:00. Closed Thanksgiving,
Christmas and New Year's Day.
ADMISSION: $3. $1.50 students (6-12). Under 5 years free.

This museum is privately supported and is part of the H. S. Colton Research Center (across the highway to the east). Most of its funds come from admission charges, gifts and memberships. It is located a few miles north of Flagstaff on U.S. 180 (See map).

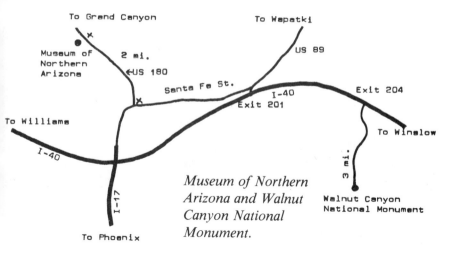

To Grand Canyon

To Wapatki

Museum of
Northern
Arizona

2 mi.

←US 180

US 89

Santa Fe St.

I-40
Exit 201

Exit 204

To Williams

To Winslow

I-40

I-17

3 mi.

Museum of Northern Arizona and Walnut Canyon National Monument.

Walnut Canyon
National Monument

To Phoenix

This well known institution has extensive exhibits pertaining mostly to the Colorado Plateau region. It also has a well stocked gift shop and bookstore. The latter also has publications of the Research Center for inspection and sale. One room is devoted to the minerals, fossils and geology of northern Arizona.

There are superior displays of prehistoric and modern Indian pottery and baskets. A time sequence on one wall highlights the position of the Sinagua in relation to the other principal cultures. Much space is devoted to Hopi and Navajo arts and crafts. One room is a fine arts museum and another is reserved for changing exhibits of the arts and crafts of modern tribes.

A view of Lomaki ruin at Wupatki National Monument.

CHAPTER 8

PATAYAN
(and others)

This could almost be called the Mystery Culture because so little is known about it and archaeologists tend to disagree among themselves concerning some of its aspects. The word is from Walapai: "the old people."

Patayan is an inclusive term that refers to a series of groups of prehistoric people who lived along the Colorado River from the Delta to Grand Canyon and extending for varying distances both east and west. Reading from south to north: Yuman, Prescott, Cerbat and Cohonina. Flooding along the Colorado for many years before Hoover Dam was completed obliterated traces of the Patayan who lived close by the river and farmed its floodplain. Most structures and artifacts have, therefore, been found at some distance from the river itself.

Dwellings ranged all the way from impermanent rock and brush shelters to pit houses to crude pueblo type villages. Pottery was mostly undecorated gray, brown or red "smudge-ware." They used metates and the usual assortment of scrapers, knives and hammerstones. Their projectile points tend toward an equilateral triangle in shape.

So far no Patayan ruin has been restored or stabilized and made available for the public to visit. It is difficult to draw a sharp boundary line between the Patayan and Hohokam desert homelands, and apparently, there was no small amount of intermingling between the cultures. One early writer even insisted that there was a Patayan "island" just a few miles north of Phoenix in the Hohokam core area—and he could be right.

In the extreme southeastern corner of Arizona (Willcox-Bisbee-Douglas) there seems to be considerable uncertainty as to who lived there. It may have been a Mogollon-Patayan—Hohokam amalgam that is difficult to identify precisely. The Amerind Foundation has investigated extensively in this area and has some interesting exhibits in its museum near Dragoon (See below).

In the Arizona midriff in the Central Highlands there is a region that may be another melding of the same cultures. There are ruins perched atop hills or on the rims of canyons that are locally referred to as "forts." And they may very well have been just that. As indicated earlier, some evidence of localized aggression does exist. Another note of interest: the author recently examined a village ruin that looked for all the world like the terraced Trincheras of northern Sonora, Mexico.

Much remains to be done in archaeological research over the entire state. Most of what is being accomplished at this time is something called salvage archaeology. This consists of surface surveys and excavations ahead of projected freeways, canals and other public works. Most of this is financed by governmental agencies or project contractors. (See ASU Anthropology Museum in Chapter 5). In the Tucson area, archaeologists are presently working ahead of the Central Arizona Project canal construction. This canal will deliver Colorado River water to portions of Pima County.

Amerind Foundation Museum, Dragoon
ADDRESS: P.O. Box 248, Dragoon, AZ 85609
TELEPHONE: (602) 586-3666
OPEN: Daily 10:00-4:00 (Telephone for June-August hours)
ADMISSION: $2. $1 children 12-18 years and Sr. Citizens
Children under 12 years free.

This is a privately administered museum, research center and art museum. It is close by I-70 between Willcox and Benson (east of Tucson). Take the Triangle T exit (318) and drive one mile southeast to access road.

Prehistoric room displays artifacts mostly from Foundation research efforts in Texas Canyon and the Willcox Playa region. Hallway exhibits of Archaic, Hohokam, Mogollon and Anasazi plus physiographic provinces.

Remainder is historic. Interesting presentations about Seri Indians of Mexico. One room is devoted entirely to Indian dances and dancers.

Kinishba ruin, an undeveloped site near Whiteriver.

CHAPTER 9

THE EXODUS

As has been related at several points throughout this book, the prehistoric Indian cultures in the state all abandoned their homes shortly before or during the 15th century. When the Spanish arrived during the 16th century, there was no trace of the Anasazi, Hohokam, Salado, etc. except their deserted dwellings.

There are strong arguments that the historic Indians may be the descendants of those who vanished. The Pima and Tohono O'odham (Papago) could be descended from the Hohokam, Salado and/or Patayan. The Zuni and Pueblo people of New Mexico might have sprung from Anasazi and/or Mogollon.

There is, however, little evidence supporting this speculation. Historic Indians do not know where they came from nor do they know the meaning (if any) of the many petroglyphs and pictographs from earlier times. Although the Hopi and Navajo have produced a variety of rock art, it is quite different from that of prehistoric times since it runs to such elements as horses and riders, trains and modern clan symbols. Historic Indian mythology throws little light upon what happened six or seven hundred years or more ago.

Why did 100,000 (more or less) individuals disappear from their homes, gardens and hunting grounds that occupied most of the state of Arizona? So far archaeologists do not have a concrete answer to this question. There are a number of hypotheses that have been offered from time to time but there is not much evidence in support of any one of them.

Climatic Changes

Climates do change and we have many choices as to why, but we do not need to be concerned with them here. There are indications of a 550-year dry-wet cycle that may have affected the Southwest enough to disrupt the lifestyles of the pre-historic inhabitants. In about 1150 a moist peak was reached and the subsequent drying trend bottomed out around 1425. Also, according to tree ring studies, there was a severe drought from 1276 to 1299. This combination may have been enough to cause a mass migration from all areas except those that were irrigating from good perennial water sources.

A change in rainfall patterns coupled with deforestation could also have been a factor where farming was done along washes or streams in canyons or valleys on the Colorado Plateau or in the Central Highlands. As long as most of the precipitation was gentle winter and spring rains or snowfall, there was no problem. If the pattern changed to the point where most of the rainfall came in the form of torrential summer thunderstorms, the results could have been disastrous.

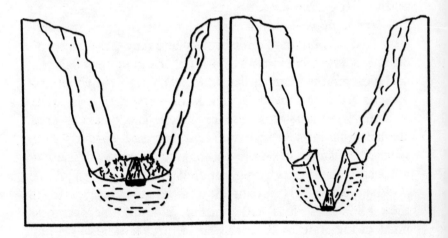

FIGURE 16. *Arroyo cutting due to climatic changes or land overuse removed rich, alluvial deposits from canyons and valleys.*

Now a process called arroyo cutting removed most of the arable land and the farmers were left with an ugly gully that could no longer be productive. Arroyo cutting has been occurring again (during the past century) in the Southwest due to over-grazing and deforestation.

Warfare

There are some indications that raiding by aggressive groups from within or outside of the area in question may have driven some or all of the people from their homes. There is not enough, however, to indicate that there was raiding and pillaging on a major scale. On the other hand, the building of easily defended cliff dwellings by Salado, Sinagua, Mogollon and Anasazi and the "fortified" villages found in western and central Arizona are themselves strong arguments. I have already mentioned the alteration of some Sinagua cliff dwellings that may have been stimulated by aggressive acts.

Even the apparently peace-loving Hohokam began building compounds with massive fort-like structures such as at Casa Grande. Again, there is little that can be pointed to in support of the warfare hypothesis.

Soil Depletion

With the exception of the Hohokam, all of the agricultural groups in Arizona farmed land that collectively amounted to a very limited acreage. After two or three hundred years of intensive agriculture on these small plots, mineral and organic depletion was inevitable. Since the Indians had no source of commercial fertilizer nor large domesticated animals to supply manure, the soil was never replenished. Lest we be quick to blame these people for their poor farming methods and disregard for their environment, remember that they had no knowledge of what they were doing; Departments of

Sacred Mountain northeast of Montezuma Well. This was a "fort" type village covering the top of the butte.

Agriculture and County Agents were still centuries away in the future.

The Hohokam had farmed their irrigated lands for at least 1000 years before the exodus. Two possibilities present themselves. The Salt River is not salty to the taste but it and the Gila, and most of their tributaries do contain relatively high concentrations of dissolved minerals. Some of these minerals no doubt supply small amounts of the minerals used by cropping. But the calcium salts leached from the rocks of the Central Highlands are very undesirable. Calcium carbonate, for instance, deposits as a form of limestone (caliche) in soil when the irrigation water evaporates. The result can be the formation of a layer of hard-pan (caliche) at a shallow depth below the soil surface. This can cause poor drainage and further salinization. Eventually it may become impossible to grow crops under these conditions.

The other possibility is that the rivers and streams may have eroded and deepened their channels to the point that the Indian diversion dams of rocks and brush could not have been built high or strong enough to get water into the canals. The droughts and dry part of the moisture cycle mentioned earlier may also have contributed by lowering the stream and river flow.

Farming and Urbanization

Paleopathology is a relatively recent development in archaeological research: the study of information revealed in the remains of ancient people—mostly their skeletons. Some abnormal physiological conditions and a variety of communicable and degenerative diseases leave their marks on the skeleton of every individual.

Surprisingly, paleopathological research has shown that the early people were better off as hunters and gatherers than as agriculturists since they enjoyed a more balanced diet of game and natural vegetable products. When they turned to farming, malnutrition became a major problem as they relied more and more upon a high carbohydrate diet (corn in the case of Arizona's prehistoric Indians). Malnutrition (not starvation) can lead to any of several nutritional deficiency diseases.

"Easy living" led to population increases that caused even more serious social and economic problems. The sedentary agricultural lifestyle resulted in people congregating in towns and villages where close living conditions and non-existent sanitary facilities and practices paved the way for the spread of communicable diseases.

To what degree these factors may have affected the Arizona cultures and the abandonment of their homes and settlements is, of course, not known at this time. We should bear in mind, however, that the hunters and gatherers survived here for at least 12,000 years whereas the agriculturists lasted for only 1500 years.

Energy Source Depletion

The only source of energy to heat dwellings and cook food available to the prehistoric people was wood. Wood for home construction and fuel had to come from the immediate area for the most part because the only available transportation was the backs of individuals.

Since wood for fuel had to be seasoned (dead and air dried for an extended time), it is probable that the Indians learned to girdle trees so that the trees would die and dry on the stump. This would have made firewood gathering much easier.

After several centuries of these kinds of practices, the fuel supply dwindled to zero because it was not practical to travel greater distances for wood. This local deforestation could have led to the drying up of springs, seeps and small streams that many localities depended upon for culinary water. Deforestation may have caused increased summer erosion of the arable land.

But, you may say, we visit these ancient ruins and there are trees all over the place. How long does it take to grow a tree? Keep in mind that it has been 600 to 800 years since the exodus; plenty of time for the forests to reestablish themselves. A 200-year-old Ponderosa Pine, for example, can be 18 inches or more in diameter and 60 or more feet tall.

Summary

It is quite probable that none of these factors was alone responsible for the abandonment. Perhaps a combination of two or more in any culture would have been enough to cause the people to move out.

Could the warring Apaches (or their forerunners) have wiped out an entire culture such as the Anasazi or the widely dispersed Mogollon? It is difficult to imagine this happening.

The exodus might have come about as a result of something the archaeologists have not yet dreamed of. Care to make a guess?

SUGGESTIONS
FOR FURTHER READING

Ambler, J. Richard, *The Anasazi,* Museum of Northern Arizona, 1977.

Barnes, F. A. and Michaelene Pendleton, *Canyon Country Prehistoric Indians,* Wasatch Publishers, Salt Lake City, 1979.

Canby, Thomas Y., "The Search for the First Americans," National Geographic, Vol. 156 No. 3, 330-363, September 1979.

Cordell, Linda S., *Prehistory of the Southwest,* The Denver Museum of Natural History, Denver, 1984.

Coronic, Halka, *Roadside Geology of Arizona,* Mountain Press, Missoula, 1983.

Gladwin, Harold S., *A History of the Ancient Southwest,* Bond Wheelwright, Portland, Maine, 1957.

Gregonis, Linda and Karl J. Reinhard, *Hohokam Indians of the Tucson Basin,* University of Arizona Press, Tucson, 1979.

Haury, Emil W., *The Hohokam, Desert Farmers and Craftsmen,* University of Arizona Press, Tucson, 1976.

McGregar, John C., *Southwestern Archaeology, Second Edition,* University of Illinois Press, Urbana, 1982.

Noble, David G., *Ancient Ruins of the Southwest,* Northland Press, Flagstaff, 1981.

Reid, J. Jefferson and David E. Doyel, *Emil W. Haury's Prehistory of the American Southwest,* University of Arizona Press, Tucson, 1986.

Schaafsma, Polly, *Indian Rock Art of the Southwest,* University of New Mexico Press, Albuquerque, 1980.

Snyder, Ernest, *Arizona Outdoor Guide,* Golden West Publishers, Phoenix, 1985.

Wormington, H. M., *Prehistoric Indians of the Southwest,* The Denver Museum of Natural History, Denver, 1947.

INDEX

THE WEST

Southwestern frontier tales more thrilling than fiction. Trimble brings history to life with humor, pathos and irony of pioneer lives: territorial politics, bungled burglaries, shady deals, frontier lawmen, fighting editors, Baron of Arizona, horse and buggy doctors, etc. *In Old Arizona* by Marshall Trimble (160 pages)...$5.00

Visit the silver cities of Arizona's golden past with this prize-winning reporter-photographer. Come along to the towns whose heydays were once wild and wicked! Crumbling adobe walls, old mines, cemeteries, cabins and castles. *Ghost Towns and Historical Haunts in Arizona* by Thelma Heatwole (144 pages)...$4.50

The American cowboy had a way with words! Lingo of the American West, captured in 2000 phrases and expressions—colorful, humorous, earthy, raunchy! Includes horse and cattle terms, rodeo talk, barb wire names, cattle brands. *Cowboy Slang* by "Frosty" Potter, illustrated by Ron Scofield (128 pages)...$5.00

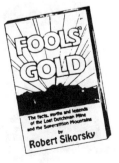

The saga of centuries-old search for Spanish gold and the Lost Dutchman Mine continues. Facts, myths and legends of fabled Superstition Mountains told by a geologist who was there. Mysteries of lost hopes, lost lives—lost gold! *Fools' Gold* by Robert Sikorsky (144 pages)...$5.00

THE WEST

Chili cookoff prize-winning recipes and regional favorites! The best of chili cookery, from mild to fiery, with and without beans. Plus a variety of taste-tempting foods made with chile peppers.

Chili-Lovers' Cook Book by Al and Mildred Fischer (128 pages) ...$3.50. *More than 50,000 copies sold!*

Ride the back trails with modern-day mountain men, as they preserve the memory of Arizona's rugged adventurers of the past. Bucksin-clad, the mountain men stage annual treks from Williams, AZ all the way to Phoenix, AZ and to other destinations. Hilarious anecdotes of hard-riding men. *Bill Williams Mountain Men* by Thomas E. Way (128 pages)...$5.00

Guide to 38 of Arizona's charming and romantic small towns and hideaways. Visit such delightful places as Ramsey Canyon, Snowflake, Bowie, Window Rock, Wickenburg, Honeymoon and a host of other idyllic Arizona wonderlands. *Arizona Hideaways* by Thelma Heatwole (128 pages)...$4.50

Outdoor enthusiasts welcome this detailed guide to plants, animals, rocks, minerals, geologic history, natural environments, landforms, resources, national forests and outdoor survival. Maps, photos, drawings, charts, index. *Arizona Outdoor Guide* by Ernest E. Snyder (126 pages)...$5.00

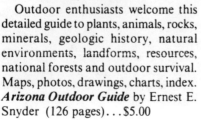

ARIZONA

Daring deeds and exploits of Wyatt Earp, Buckey O'Neill, the Rough Riders, Arizona Rangers, cowboys, Power brothers shootout, notorious Tom Horn, Pleasant Valley wars, the Hopi revolt—action-packed true tales of early Arizona!

Arizona Adventure by Marshall Trimble (160 pages)...$5.00

Take the back roads to and thru Arizona's natural wonders—Canyon de Chelly, Wonderland of Rocks, Monument Valley, Rainbow Bridge, Four Peaks, Swift Trail, Alamo Lake, Virgin River Gorge, Palm Canyon, Red Rock Country! *Arizona—off the beaten path!* by Thelma Heatwole (144 pages)...$4.50

A taste of the Old Southwest, from sizzling Indian fry bread to prickly pear marmalade, from sourdough biscuits to refried beans, from beef jerky to cactus candy.

Arizona Cook Book by Al and Mildred Fischer (144 pages)...$3.50. *More than 100,000 copies sold!*

Discover arrowheads, old coins, bottles, fossil beds, old forts, petroglyphs, ruins, lava tubes, waterfalls, ice caves, cliff dwellings and other Arizona wonders. Detailed maps and text invite you to visit 60 hidden, out-of-the-way places. *Explore Arizona!* by Rick Harris (128 pages)...$5.00